Music Education
of the Future

OTHER BOOKS BY DAVID WHITWELL

Philosophic Foundations of Education
Foundations of Music Education
Music Education of the Future
The Sousa Oral History Project

The History and Literature of the Wind Band and Wind Ensemble Series
A Concise History of the Wind Band
Volume 1 The Wind Band and Wind Ensemble Before 1500
Volume 2 The Renaissance Wind Band and Wind Ensemble
Volume 3 The Baroque Wind Band and Wind Ensemble
Volume 4 The Wind Band and Wind Ensemble of the Classic Period (1750–1800)
Volume 5 The Nineteenth-Century Wind Band and Wind Ensemble

For a complete list of the currently available works of David Whitwell visit:
whitwellbooks.com

David Whitwell

Music Education of the Future

EDITED BY CRAIG DABELSTEIN

WHITWELL BOOKS • AUSTIN, TEXAS, USA

MUSIC EDUCATION OF THE FUTURE
DAVID WHITWELL
EDITED BY CRAIG DABELSTEIN
WWW.WHITWELLBOOKS.COM

WHITWELL BOOKS
P.O. BOX 342673
AUSTIN, TEXAS, USA

Copyright © David Whitwell 2011
All rights reserved

Composed in Bembo Book
Published in the United States of America

MUSIC EDUCATION OF THE FUTURE (PAPERBACK) ISBN 978-1-936512-11-9

Contents

Foreword   vii

Preface   xi

1. On The Roots Of Music Education   1

2. Thoughts on the Perception of Music   15

3. Purpose and Meaning in Music Education   31

4. Music Education Must Be Experiential   47

5. Music Education Must Educate All Children   63

6. Music Education Must Educate the Real Child   73

7. Two Paramount New Purposes   109

8. Epilogue   149

Illustrations   153

About the Author   157

Foreword

I recently spoke to a 13-year-old student who just started Year 8 at the high school where I teach music. I asked her if she was going to sign up to play an instrument in the music program. 'No,' she answered, 'I don't like music.'

'Do you have an iPod?' I asked.

'Of course,' she answered.

'What's on it?' I asked. Her eyes brightened considerably as she rattled off the names of many artists and songs (all of which an 'old' person like me had never heard of, of course!).

And this is the point so many music teachers miss. All students, *all people the world over*, love music—it's in our DNA. And in the most overwhelming case of irony, it is *music* teachers who dissuade students from studying music.

Why did that student say she didn't like music when she clearly does? It was the experience she had in her primary school ensemble that she didn't like, and being a 13-year-old, she tarred all music teachers and music programs with the same brush. I would guess that in her primary school ensemble the conductor did more talking than the students did playing. I also assume that the repertoire was, to put it as politely as possible, forgettable. That student did not get an artistic experience (yes, even at the primary school or beginner level, students can have an artistic experience—frankly, it is the only type of experience they should have!). Had this student had a positive, exciting, and artistic experience in her primary school she certainly would not be giving up music at the age of thirteen.

Imagine this scenario …

A student comes to your office and says, 'I want to play the saxophone.' [Notice that the student said 'play' the saxophone, not 'learn about' the saxophone.] The saxophone teacher spends a lesson or two showing the student how to set up the instrument, where to put it in the storeroom, how to adjust the height of the music stand, how to put the reed on, how to take the reed off, where to put the reed once you've taken it off. Then come the note names, where they sit on the staff, what the fingering is, how long the note lasts for, how loud to play it, what to do with your tongue ...

A couple of weeks have gone by and the student cannot play even a simple song (such as *Mary had a little lamb*) for her parents yet. Would you persist with something you love if the teacher was, to all appearances, trying their best to destroy everything you like about it? No. You would find your own way to experience it, and for our students that means withdrawing to a world of headphones, iPods and Guitar Hero. This is what you call *discouraging* a student from playing music.

But wait—I can hear band directors and music teachers the world over: 'Students need to know these things!' Of course they do, but it is the primary role of music teachers to nurture the students' love of music, not kill it. It is the role of music teachers to balance the theoretical with the practical, and where possible, emphasise the practical, the experiential, over any theory.

Ask yourself, 'Does the student really need to know this to play it? To enjoy it? To feel it? To make the audience feel it?' If not, then to quote Dr. Whitwell, spend your time teaching *music*, not teaching *about* music.

When most readers see the title of this book, *Music Education of the Future*, they will envisage keyboard labs, laptop computers, smart whiteboards, play-a-long and assessment software—all of the things in which the technologically savvy music teacher is adept. How disappointed they'll be when they start reading about Plato, Aristotle, Montaigne, and bicameral brain function. However, it is through this thorough study of the past as well as of recent neurological discoveries that Dr. Whitwell has been able to confidently articulate a vision for the future of music education.

Since reading this volume it seems to me that many music curricula are written with a very limited perspective on the *potential* of music study. David Whitwell has absorbed four thousand years of commentary on music education and has compared the successful factors of each era, and from them created a theory of music education of the future that, for me, is beautiful in its sense of inevitability—to read his volumes on music education is to come to the realisation that music education should be no other way.

Music Education of the Future concludes Dr. David Whitwell's three-volume series (following *Philosophic Foundations of Education* and *Foundations of Music Education*) and advocates a music education pedagogy that teaches music, not one that is obsessed with the teaching of concepts. This book does not offer the quick fix that so many band directors and music teachers desire. It offers a new way of thinking about teaching and conducting; a new philosophy. It will require enthusiasm from passionate music teachers to influence their school administrators, politicians, and parent bodies that playing music is important. The only people who don't need convincing are the students. They've been trying to tell us forever.

Craig Dabelstein
Brisbane, 2011

Preface

A NEW SCHOOL YEAR IS ABOUT TO BEGIN and a large group of children approach the school building to begin the First Grade. They arrive with varying prior introductions to reading, writing and social skills but the single thing they all have in common is a love for music. Imagine what this should mean for the music teacher. Suppose you were a geology teacher and someone told you that all children loved geology before they even entered the building to begin the First Grade. What would that do for your enthusiasm as a geology teacher? How would that change your initial lesson plans? Would not the fact that the children already love geology not inspire you to immediately go right to the heart of the discipline?

Unfortunately, for geology teachers this is only a dream. But it is true for music teachers and how do they respond to these new young faces who already love music? They turn their backs on them and they do not teach music. Instead they teach about music, they teach a concept-based description of music. No other one of our teaching colleagues can get away with this. The math teacher must teach math. The Spanish teacher cannot avoid teaching Spanish. The reading teacher wants to teach reading, not etymology. Why would a music teacher not want to teach music? How did the field of Music Education come to describe itself as something it is not?

What do we mean by this? What these young students learn about music before they enter the school building for the first time is a truth which everyone on earth understands as a matter of common sense: Music is a special language of feeling. They come to understand this definition of music by themselves for two reasons: the basic emotions are universal and in place before birth and because essential tools to understand music are genetic. It is for these two reasons that we hear that familiar phrase, 'Music is the International Language.' Actually, this familiar phrase is incomplete and should read, 'Music is the International Language of Feeling.'

In America music teachers do not teach the fundamental nature of music, music as a language of feeling. They do not do this even though four decades of medical research (including a Nobel Prize in Medicine) has confirmed and stressed the importance of music as the most powerful language of our experiential selves. They do not do this even though using music to introduce and identify the individual emotions of the student presents the Golden Opportunity for music education to contribute something to education at large which nothing else in the school building can do. They do not do this even though nearly three thousand years of discussion by the greatest of the world's philosophers have emphasized the fact that the performance of music is the language of feeling. What else do music educators think Plato meant when he defined music as 'a science of the phenomena of love in [its] application to harmony and rhythm.'

The importance of feeling, so recognized in the ancient world, came to an impassible barrier in the early Roman Church who wanted to remove emotion from the lives of the early Christians. The fourth century St. Basil wrote that a good Christian should not even laugh, for laughing is a form of emotion! After the Church had closed the schools and then later reopened them they had to find some way of including music in the curriculum but without reference to emotion. So they made music a category of arithmetic, made sure that all music treatises for the next one thousand years were written by mathematicians and not musicians and created our notational system in which, even today, there is not a single symbol to represent any kind of emotion.

No matter how powerful the Church was, there must have been plenty of people who knew that it was ridiculous to maintain that music is mathematics. So the Church said, OK, we will teach the intellectual aspects ('speculative music') of music, that is to say theory, in the schools and we will leave performance ('practical music') to the musicians out in the streets. Not only did centuries of later philosophers debate this artificial division of music, but traces of this division can still be seen in every university music department today.

Where philosophers of music education have failed us, the medical profession has come forward during the past four decades to confirm the truth of the role and value of music to our species and to consequently offer to any unbiased observer a beacon light to illuminate the centuries of nonsense which followed the Church's attempt to denigrate feelings. The last portion of this book represents my personal attempt to urge music educators to make a great contribution to civilization by returning to the idea of teaching music as music and by beginning to build a music curriculum that helps children develop their understanding of their personal emotional template and to reduce concepts and data to their proper adjunct role.

                David Whitwell
                Austin, Texas

I On the Roots of Music Education

THE NATURE OF MUSIC EDUCATION has its basis in the physiological relationship of music to our species. We might therefore begin by asking, 'How old is Music?' Charles Darwin not only believed it very old, but believed the emotions we feel in hearing music today are a bridge to very remote ancestors.

> Music has a wonderful power ... of recalling in a vague and indefinite manner, those strong emotions which were felt during long-past ages, when, as is probable, our early progenitors courted each other by the aid of vocal tones.[1]

Our oldest extant records of music are in the prehistoric cave paintings of France and Spain, where we not only see musicians pictured but the visible prints of dancing feet, suggesting that music was involved in the rituals associated with these paintings. Contemporary with these caves are the Cro-Magnon humans, who played on percussion instruments made from mammoth bones, in addition to the flute-types pictured in the caves, so it seems clear these people were musical. They must have been perceptive listeners as well, for it has been observed that the most resonant caves have the most paintings.

Much more recent are the oldest surviving specimens of actual instruments. They are of a nature which one might associate with very early man, as they are all made from natural objects—flutes of clay, tree branches and bones; percussion instruments from shells; and trumpet-types from large sea shells. Curiously, there are surviving clay flutes with holes cut for *diatonic* pitches which are thousands of years older than Pythagoras, to whom we give credit for 'discovering' the over-

A portrait of 31-year-old Charles Darwin by George Richmond

[1] Charles Darwin, *The Expression of Emotions in Man and Animals* [1872] (New York: St Martin's Press, 1979), 219; also *The Descent of Man*, II, 336.

Bone flute dated in the Upper Paleolithic from Geissenklösterle, a German cave on the Swabian region

tone series. How is this possible? The answer is that Pythagoras only worked out the mathematics of describing the overtone series, while the overtone series itself, as a genuine physical law of nature, was of course always present. Early man needed to be able to hear only the fourth overtone to be able to be in touch with the principle of the major key tonal system.

Simple vocal sounds reflecting emotions would logically seem to be the first recognizable oral sounds, as is suggested by Richard Cytowic, MD:

> Consciousness, language, and higher mental functions are the *consequences of our ability to express emotion*.[2]

Richard Wagner, among others, suggested that these simple vocal sounds[3] uttered in succession became melodic in character.

> The primal organ of utterance of the inner man, however, is music, as the most spontaneous expression of the inner feeling stimulated from without. A mode of expression similar to that still proper to the beasts was alike first employed by man [and this we can demonstrate at any moment] by removing from our language its dumb articulations [consonants] and leaving nothing but the open sounds [of the vowels]. In these vowels, if we think of them as stripped of their consonants, and picture to ourselves the manifold and vivid play of inner feelings, with all their range of joy and sorrow, we shall obtain an image of man's first emotional language; a language in which the stirred and high-strung Feeling could certainly express itself through nothing but a combination of ringing tones, which altogether of itself must take the form of Melody. This melody, which was accompanied by appropriate bodily gestures in such a way as the gestures would also appear a simultaneous inner expression, and from these gestures we get rhythm.[4]

The great language scholar, Otto Jespersen, points out that in passionate speech the voice still tends toward pitch fluctuation, that civilization attempts to reduce this effect by reducing passionate utterance and that savages still use a sing-song manner of speaking.

> These facts and considerations all point to the conclusion that there was once a time when all speech was song, or rather when these two actions were not yet differentiated.[5]

[2] Richard Cytowic, MD, *The Man who Tasted Shapes* (New York: Putnam, 1993), 196.

[3] All modern languages use the same five vowel sounds.

Richard Wagner, Paris, 1860

[4] Ashton Ellis, *The Prose Works of Richard Wagner* (New York: Broude), II, 224ff.

[5] Otto Jespersen, *Language: Its Nature, Development and Origin* (New York: Henry Holt, 1922), 420. Deryck Cooke, *The Language of Music* (Oxford: Oxford University Press, 1990), 26, observes that in some cases little differentiation yet exists:
> A groan of 'Ah!' uttered by a character in an opera on a two-note phrase of definite pitch is hardly different from a groan of 'Ah!' uttered by a character in a play at indefinite pitch; the effect is equally emotive in both cases.

Perhaps the strongest evidence for this theory that music preceded language is found in the fact that we still form melodic contours with each sentence we 'speak' today. In this regard, Roger Bacon (b. ca. 1214), made the interesting comment that 'accent is a kind of singing.'[6]

This topic continued to hold great interest for later philosophers. The fifteenth-century Scholastic philosopher, Nicholas of Cusa, found it interesting that lower animals still communicate emotions by vowel-like sounds.[7] The impressive French writer, Jean-Baptiste Du Bos (1670–1742), placed great importance in the relationship of vocal sounds with Nature herself. It is a particularly important point he makes when he reminds his readers that spoken words are mere symbols of emotion, but carry no actual emotional content in themselves. Sung words, on the other hand, carry the direct emotional meaning of the music.

[6] *The Opus Majus of Roger Bacon*, trans., Robert Burke (New York: Russell & Russell, 1962), I, 259ff.

[7] Nicholas of Cusa, 'Compendium,' XIV, trans., William Wertz, Jr., in *Toward a New Council of Florence* (Washington, D.C.: Schiller Institute, 1993), 539ff.

> Just as the painter imitates the forms and colors of nature so the musician imitates the tones of the voice—its accents, sighs and inflections. He imitates in short all the sounds that nature herself uses to express the feelings and passions. All these sounds, as we have already shown, have a wonderful power to move us because they are the signs of the passions that are the work of nature herself, from whence they have derived their energy. Spoken words, on the other hand are only arbitrary symbols of the passions.[8]

[8] Jean-Baptiste Du Bos, *Réflexions critiques sur la poësie et sur la peinture* [Paris, 1719], quoted in Peter le Huray and James Day, *Music and Aesthetics in the Eighteenth and Early-Nineteenth Centuries* (Cambridge: Cambridge University Press, 1981), 18.

Voltaire, who was very interested in this topic, suggested that language began with simple emotional utterances which were later clarified by the addition of gesture.

> May we not, without offending anyone, suppose that the alphabet originated in cries and exclamations? Infants of themselves articulate one sound when an object catches their attention, another when they laugh, and a third when they are whipped, which they ought not to be …
>
> From exclamations formed by vowels as natural to children as croaking is to frogs, the transition to a complete alphabet is not so great as may be thought. A mother must always have said to her child the equivalent of come, go, take, leave, hush!, etc. These words represent nothing; they describe nothing; but a gesture makes them intelligible.

He adds that he is astonished when he reflects on the ages it must have taken to go from this to sentences. He concludes his discussion by observing that as words were invented they soon

4 MUSIC EDUCATION OF THE FUTURE

became charged with subjective inferences, from their association with religion, from magic, from necromancy, etc., thus losing their value as invariable symbols. Thus, he says, 'the alphabet was the origin of all man's knowledge, and of all his errors.'[9]

William Shenstone (1714–1763) seemed to suggest that instead of saying speech developed after music, perhaps we should regard speech as a form of music.

> Harmony of period and melody of style have greater weight than is generally imagined in the judgment we pass upon writing and writers. As proof of this, let us reflect, what texts of scripture, what lines in poetry, or what periods we most remember and quote, either in verse or prose, and we shall find them to be only musical ones.[10]

How old, then, is Music? Perhaps it is so ancient that we should perhaps think of its origin in biological terms. A very interesting proposal in this regard has been made by the French doctor, Alfred A. Tomatis. He once lived near the Solesmes monastery known to all musicians for their work in the notation of chant early in the last century. This Order, which today engages in agriculture work, had for centuries maintained the practice of chanting six hours a day. A new head man, an efficiency expert, proposed to the brothers that if they reduced their chanting to two hours a day they would have four additional hours for agriculture work and could

[9] The discussion is found under 'The Alphabet,' in his *Philosophical Dictionary*.

[10] William Shenstone, *Men and Manners* (Boston: Houghton Mifflin, 1927), 49.

Portrait bust of William Shenstone from the frontispiece of 'The Works in Verse and Prose of William Shenstone, Esq.,' Vol. I, Second Edition (London, J Dodsley, 1765)

Abbey of Solesmes, seen from the Port of Solesmes, Sarthe, France

Gregorian chants for the night office of Christmas, Monastery of Solesmes, 1895

thereby increase their income for needs of the monastery. So they began doing this and after a period of time they all began to get sick. A local doctor was called in, but could find nothing wrong. An engineer was called to check ventilation, etc., but could find nothing. Finally Tomatis volunteered to come by, looked everything over, and suggested they return to six hours of chanting. They did and they all got well, and of course accomplished more work in less time as a result of being well.

Tomatis then began to reflect on the fact that so many societies engage in some sort of chanting, began to wonder why this should be and began to study chanting throughout the world. He finally offered the proposition that perhaps music is a kind of 'food' for the brain, that it 'warms up' the brain for enhanced activity. A similar conclusion had been made by Disraeli, during the nineteenth century, when he observed that 'Music is a stimulant to mental exertion.' There is some clinical evidence for this kind of physical impact on the brain by music, for we know listening to music can cause the pleasant release of endorphins. Perhaps such dimly felt physical associations with music, together with the ancient observation that music is the only Art you cannot see, help explain why music from the earliest times was thought to have some association with the divine.[11]

One physicist believes that music is so ancient as to be related to the very essence of nature itself.

> Analyzing music from many different cultures and historical periods, Richard Voss of IBM's Thomas J. Watson Research Center found that a simple mathematical relationship describes how the notes of any musical piece rise and fall in relation to the composition as a whole. This same mathematical relationship is also found in a wide variety of other natural patterns, such as the changes in the electrical patterns of brain cells, the fluctuations in sunspots and the growing of tree rings …
>
> Voss's research suggests that the essence of music may be its subtle reflection of nature.[12]

Music, he says, is as old as nature. Perhaps so, for modern physics has discovered that every organ of the body, even every molecule, atom and subatomic particle actually vibrates to specific pitches which can be heard under great amplification. One of these physicists, Dr. Hans Jenny of Switzerland, believed that it is the combination of these pitches, our har-

[11] The civilization of Sumeria, ca. 3,000 BC, is the earliest one we know which had developed a sophisticated tradition of music. Since they believed music was of divine origin, they created temples for a number of gods, all of whom they believed had to be entertained, to keep them in good spirits, by singing and playing of instruments. Among these gods was one called *Enlil*, the father of humanity, who governed with a musical instrument called *al*. [See Alfred Sendrey, *Music in the Social and Religious Life of Antiquity* (Rutherford: Fairleigh Dickson University Press, 1974), 31]

[12] 'The Musical Brain,' op. cit.

mony if you will, which, together with gravity, accounts for our body being shaped as it is.[13] It has been further suggested that, since we are made up of these vibrating systems, many health problems may have some relationship to our literally being 'out-of-tune.' Is this also why we use expressions such as muscle *tone*? Or we say, 'She is *in tune* with everyone,' or '*I am disconcerted*,' or '*I am in concert with that decision*' and why Aristotle once said, 'Beauty is visible harmony.' We should also mention that the late fifteenth-century scholar, Franchino Gaffurio, in his *Theorica musice*, quotes a remarkable passage from Cicero, who had apparently reached this same idea by deduction.

> A certain tuning pitch exists in one's body like that of the voice and instruments called harmony; just as sounds are made in singing, so out of the nature and form of the whole body issue various vibrations.[14]

So, if our very molecules and atoms produce pitches, then music must be older than them. Perhaps it was the pitch created by the vibration of the rotation of the earth which stirred that primordial 'soup' that began the chain of evolution. A vibrating pitch may have been the mid-wife of us all!

In view of this physiological connection between man and his music, it should perhaps be no surprise that many early philosophers believed that music was both genetic and universal in character. 'Why,' Aristotle asks, 'do all men love music?'

> Is it because we naturally rejoice in natural movements? This is shown by the fact that children rejoice in [rhythm and melody] as soon as they are born. Now we delight in the various types of melody for their moral character, but we delight in rhythm because it contains a familiar and ordered number and moves in a regular manner; for ordered movement is naturally more akin to us than disordered, and is therefore more in accordance with nature.[15]

The first century AD philosopher, Philodemus of Gadara, not only recognized the universality of music, but suspected that this universality was genetic in origin as well.

> We have an innate affinity with the Muses, one which does not have to be learned. This is clearly shown by the way infants are lulled to sleep with wordless singing.[16]

---

[13] This reminds us that some ancient Greeks thought of the lyre as a symbol of the human form, with strings representing the nerves and the player the spirit. See Manly P. Hall, *The Secret Teachings of All Ages* (Los Angeles: The Philosophical Research Society, 1972), 81-83.

[14] 'Tusculan Disputations,' 1.9.19-20, quoted in Paolo Cortese, 'De cardinalatu libri tres,' quoted in Nino Pirrotta, in *Music and Culture in Italy from the Middle Ages to the Baroque* (Cambridge: Harvard University Press, 1984), 177ff.

[15] *Problemata*, 920b.28.

[16] Quoted in Warren D. Anderson, *Ethos and Education in Greek Music* (Cambridge: Harvard University Press, 1966), 173.

Erasmus (1469–1536) also found the effect of music on children to be evidence of innate understanding.

> [This is its nature] just as children too are affected by the modes of music through some natural affinity, even when they have no idea what music is.[17]

Believing that everything was made by God, it is no surprise to find the early Church fathers also mentioning the innate understanding of music found in man. St. John Chrysostom argued that the pleasure man finds in music is divinely implanted.[18] St. Augustine makes a similar argument, discussing it from the perspective of both players and the listening public.

> AUGUSTINE. How do you explain the fact that an ignorant crowd hisses off a flute player letting out futile sounds, and on the other hand applauds one who sings well, and finally that the more agreeably one sings the more fully and intensely it is moved? For it isn't possible to believe the crowd does all this by the art of music, is it?
> STUDENT. No.
> AUGUSTINE. How then?
> STUDENT. I think it is done by nature giving everyone a sense of hearing by which such things are judged.
> AUGUSTINE. You are right.[19]

The great Italian Renaissance theorist, Zarlino, thought it might be some genetic memory of the music of the angels which impels man to sing as a means of easing labor.

> Many were of the opinion that in this life every soul is won by music, and, although the soul is imprisoned by the body, it still remembers and is conscious of the music of the heavens, forgetting every hard and annoying labor.[20]

This idea of the genetic understanding of music being a kind of memory in us, was also mentioned by the great German philosopher, Gottfried Wilhelm Leibniz (1646–1716). He believed genetic knowledge explained why 'we need only the beginning of a song to remember it,'[21] and why hearing a musical performance seems to create 'a sympathetic echo in us.'[22]

[17] 'Adages,' in *The Collected Works of Erasmus* (Toronto: University of Toronto Press, 1992), XXXI, 167.

[18] St. John Chrysostom, 'Exposition of Psalm XLI,' quoted in Oliver Strunk, *Source Readings in Music History* (New York: Norton, 1950), 68.

[19] *On Music*, trans., Robert Taliaferro in *Writings of Saint Augustine* (New York: Fathers of the Church), I, v.

[20] 'Le Istitutioni harmoniche.'

[21] Leibniz, *New Essays Concerning Human Understanding*, in Leroy Loemker, *Philosophical Papers and Letters* (Dordrecht: Reidel, 1956), preface.

[22] Leibniz, 'On Wisdom' (c. 1690-1698), in ibid., 425ff.

The Baroque writers tended to concentrate on the genetic understanding of specific elements of music. The brilliant thinker, Jean-Philippe Rameau (1683–1764), was absorbed for years with the idea that man is born with a genetic pitch template, something which modern research seems also to suggest.[23] In 1734, Rameau was clearly pondering observations which he had made along these lines.

> In music the ear obeys only nature. It takes account of neither measure nor range. Instinct alone leads it.
>
> Whether a novice or the most experienced person in music, the moment one sings an improvisation, one ordinarily places the first tone in the middle register of the voice and then continues up, even though the voice range above or below this first tone is about equal; this is completely consistent with the resonance of any sounding body from which all emanating overtones are above its fundamental tone which one thinks one is hearing alone.
>
> On the other hand, inexperienced as one may be, one hardly ever fails, when improvising on an instrument, immediately to play, ever ascending, the perfect chord made up of the overtones of the sounding body, the major form of which is always preferred to the minor, unless the latter is suggested by some reminiscence.[24]

Twenty-five years later he was still struggling with this idea. He begins by discounting the ancient explanations based on faith and wonders why these early philosophers did not pursue natural rules, that is, understanding based on Nature.

> [The ancient writers] found the relationships between sounds in divinely inspired order; they discoursed a great deal on that subject, and every reason they were able to advance evaporated like a wisp of smoke. Finally the geometricians and the philosophers became disheartened. Can it be true that up to the present time man has always been so enthralled by this single inspiration that it never occurred to anyone to seek the reason why, despite ourselves, we should be compelled to prefer certain intervals to others after certain sounds, especially after the first sound? Allow your natural feelings to operate in yourself with no preconceived expectation and then try to see if you can ever ascend a semitone after a given semitone, and whether you can do the same thing after two successive tones. Why was this suggested to me in this way? Whence this sensation? What could have given rise to this sensation in me, if it was not in the moment itself? It was necessary to test the effect of the sound, and from it three sounds would have been distinguished which form that enchanting harmony, and from there one would have proceeded with certainty, as I believe I have done.

[23] St. Augustine, in his treatise, *On Music*, also suspected a genetic template.
> I believe, while we were discussing these things, a fifth kind appeared from somewhere, a kind in the natural judgment of perceiving when we are delighted by the equality of numbers or offended at a flaw in them. [See *On Music*, trans., Robert Taliaferro in *Writings of Saint Augustine* (New York: Fathers of the Church), VI, iv]

[24] Jean Philippe Rameau, *Observations sur notre instinct pour la musique et sur son principe* (1734), quoted in Sam Morgenstern, *Composers on Music* (New York: Pantheon, 1956), 44.

Jean-Philippe Rameau

The principle is inexhaustible and holds true for theology as well as geometry and physics. Anyone more enlightened than myself should be able to draw the most far-reaching conclusions from this and already I can envision the origin of that final knowledge which cannot be denied without denying the phenomenon from which it is derived.[25]

Another French composer of the Baroque, Michel de Saint-Lambert, in his *Les Principes du Clavecin* of 1702, adds rhythm to pitch as genetic information. After briefly mentioning some of the abilities needed in performance, he says,

> Though this at first sight may appear a large order, it is nevertheless sure that this extreme accuracy in intonation and rhythm is a gift given to almost all men, like sight and speech. There are very few who do not sing and dance naturally; if it is not with the delicacy and correctness that Art has sought, it is at least with the correctness which Art dictates and which Art itself has derived from Nature. It is already a great asset for those who want to learn music or to play some instrument that they know they have discernment of the ear by nature, that is, the first and most important of these aptitudes.[26]

The French philosopher, Charles Batteaux (1713–1780), in reference to the innate character of music, quotes, without source, a Latin expression, 'We are led to melody by natural instinct.'[27]

Modern medical research has identified in more specific terms the nature of the musical information we carry genetically into birth. For one thing, there is pitch awareness itself, which must have been critical to early man. The actual affinity for a musical language can also be tested at a very early age. Dennis Molfese of the University of Pennsylvania has conducted studies on infants less than forty-eight hours after birth.[28] University of California researchers believe that infants are born with a genetic ability to recognize and respond to music, even before language.[29] Psychologists have found that even before age *one*, infants can detect errors in music![30] Among the most interesting findings are those which have to do with the acquisition of 'perfect pitch.'

> There is evidence that almost all musicians who began their training before the age of 6 possess absolute pitch, compared with none of those who began after the age of 11.[31]

[25] Letter to A. M. Beguillet, October 6, 1762, quoted in Gertrude Norman and Miriam Shrifte, *Letters of Composers* (New York, Knopf, 1946), 20.

[26] Michel de Saint-Lambert, *Les Principes du Clavecin* (1702), quoted in Carol MacClintock, *Readings in the History of Music in Performance* (Bloomington: Indiana University Press, 1979), 212.

[27] Charles Batteux (1713-1780), *Les beaux-arts réduits à un même principe* [Paris,1746], quoted in Peter le Huray and James Day, *Music and Aesthetics in the Eighteenth and Early-Nineteenth Centuries* (Cambridge: Cambridge University Press, 1981), 50ff.

[28] Craig Buck, 'Knowing the LEFT from the RIGHT,' *Human Behavior*, June, 1976.

[29] *Associated Press*, January 23, 1992.

[30] 'The Musical Brain,' *U. S. News & World Report*, June 11, 1990.

[31] D. Sergeant, 'Experimental Investigation of Absolute Pitch,' in *Journal of Research in Musical Education*, 1969, 17, 135-143.

Research by Dr. Jamshed Bharucha, of Dartmouth College has found that we have a biological affinity for *melodic patterns*. It is interesting that this idea of genetic preference for certain kinds of melody was mentioned by the great English philosopher, Thomas Hobbes (1588–1679).

> That which pleases is called a tune [*air*]; but for what reason one succession in tone and measure is a more pleasing tune than another, I confess I know not; but I conjecture the reason to be, for that some of them imitate and revive some passion which otherwise we take no notice of, and the other not.[32]

32 'Human Nature,' VIII, 2.

This biological affinity for musical patterns is present in the brains of other species as well. A study by Stewart Hulse of Johns Hopkins University found that starlings have the ability to recognize a simple melody in different keys, and other studies suggest that dolphins recognize octaves. In another experiment, pigeons were trained to distinguished random excerpts of music by J. S. Bach from excerpts by Igor Stravinsky, and they were even able to correctly categorize music by other composers as being either 'Bach-like' or 'Stravinsky-like'.[33]

33 'The Musical Brain,' *U. S. News & World Report*, June 11, 1990.

Jay Dowling, of the University of Texas at Dallas, has discovered clinical evidence to suggest that ordinary people perceive these melodic patterns on the basis of the relationship between the notes themselves, and not on the basis of precise pitches. Thus, almost everybody can sing 'Happy Birthday' starting from any note on the piano.[34] But, with bad news for the twelve-tone composers, research by John Pierce at Stanford has demonstrated that the brain has little ability to recognize melodic patterns played backwards. For example, most people don't realize that the sound of the word *we* is the reverse of the sound of *you*.[35]

34 ibid.

35 ibid.

It would seem, then, that there is a great deal about the nature of music which cannot be explained as a learned art. And if none of this research existed, the point would still be obvious in the fact that people all over the world listen to music, even though they 'know' nothing at all about music.

Finally, there is the fundamental issue of the two hemispheres of our brain, a bicameral nature found already in the very earliest of ancient fossils. Every reader must be familiar with the medical research of the past forty years, research which won the Nobel Prize in medicine, on the left and right hemispheres of the brain. While more recent research suggests there is some cross-over possible, nevertheless it does appear that the left hemisphere is best adapted for rational activity and the right hemisphere for non-rational activity. Written music, like any symbolic language, is found in the left; music performed, being experiential, is understood in the right.[36] While the most recent clinical findings suggest this is more complex in the brain, nothing yet departs from the basic division I have suggested.

These findings answer many questions, such as why it is difficult to *talk* about music or to write an adequate love letter, why Erasmus observed that one cannot listen to music if someone is talking[37] and why he also observed 'My tongue is not adequate to my feelings'[38] and why Martin Luther found he could not write while his son, Hans, was singing.[39] Much is also explained by the fact that the left hemisphere (the talking and writing half) does not recognize the existence of the right hemisphere and therefore does not understand the world of the right hemisphere. Blaise Pascal (1623–1662) was thus prompted to comment,

> The heart has its reason, which reason does not know. We feel it in a thousand things.[40]

If we remember the fact that our left hemisphere controls the right hand and the right hemisphere the left, then we understand why the Indians of the American Southwest distinguished between the functions of the hands, the right for writing and the left for music, and why the French word for Law, one of the most conceptual, logical and left hemisphere oriented of professions, is *droit* ('Right,' as in right hand). For the same reason we have the traditional phrases 'He received a *left*-handed compliment,' or the more positive, 'The Favorite sat on the *right*-hand of the King.' Since sight and hearing cross to opposite brains, similar to the operation of the hands, we find most remarkable indeed a poem by Thomas Sheridan (1687–1738), a priest and schoolmaster friend of Swift. He was absolutely, and astonishingly, correct in his assigning of right or left eye and ear functions vis-a-vis their actual relationship with the brain hemispheres.

---

[36] See Craig Buck, 'Knowing the LEFT from the RIGHT,' in *Human Behavior*, June, 1976. Some research suggests that trained musicians who listen for conceptual detail hear music with the left hemisphere. Thus, among other things, music schools ruin musicians as listeners.

[37] 'The Tongue,' [1525] in *The Collected Works of Erasmus* (Toronto: University of Toronto Press, 1992), XXIX, 279.

[38] 'A Congratulatory Poem [for] Prince Philip, Upon his Happy Return,' in ibid., LXXXV, 139.

[39] In a conversation of 1532 reported by Veit Dietrich, in *Luther's Works* (St. Louis: Concordia, 1961), LIV, 21.

[40] Blaise Pascal, *Pensées* (New York: Modern Library, 1941), III, 277.

> With my left eye, I see you sit snug in your stall,
> With my right I'm attending the lawyers that scrawl.
> With my left I behold your bellower a cur chase;
> With my right I'm reading my deeds for a purchase.
> My left ear's attending the hymns of the choir,
> My right ear is stunned with the noise of the crier.[41]

Since some remain concerned over the sometimes confusing and conflicting data of this research, perhaps for the moment we might simply all agree that man has his rational and experiential sides of his personality, however they are organized physiologically. Certainly this aspect of man has been observed and commented on by a wide range of writers. Roger Bacon (b. ca. 1214) wrote of the two sides of man being the 'cogitative faculty' and that of 'experience.'[42] There were several fifteenth-century works of English literature which explored 'Reson and Sensuallyte.' Francis Bacon (1561–1626) believed the brain to be divided into understanding and reason on one hand, and appetite and affection on the other.[43] And Wagner wrote at some length on 'understanding' versus 'feeling.'[44] In another place, Wagner observed,

> The Understanding tells us: '*So it is*,'—only when the Feeling has told us: '*So it must be*.'[45]

Each of these two sides of our personality has its own form of communication. The 'understanding side' has language. The 'feeling side' has music. We choose between language and music depending on what we wish to communicate. Language, numbers, books and stage plays communicate rational thought through language. Music communicates feeling.

---

[41] Quoted in *The Poetical Works of Jonathan Swift* (London: Bell and Daldy, n.d.), III, 245.

[42] 'Experimental Science,' in *The Opus Majus of Roger Bacon*, trans., Robert Burke (New York: Russell & Russell, 1962), I.

[43] *The Works of Francis Bacon* (Cambridge: Cambridge University Press, 1869), VI, 258ff.

[44] 'A Communication to my Friends,' in William Ellis, *Wagner's Prose Works* (New York: Broude), I, 271ff.

[45] 'The Play and Dramatic Poetry,' in ibid., II, 209.

2 *Thoughts on the Perception of Music*

ANY DISCUSSION OF BRAIN ACTIVITY is made difficult first of all by the subject's very complexity and second in the fact that even in those cases where we appear to have begun to understand a specific function there can be found individuals who seem to be constructed entirely differently and do not conform to the model. In the case of the perception of music, this strange variety has been wonderfully demonstrated in Oliver Sacks' book, *Musicophilia*.[1] Sacks, a physician and neurologist, documents here that among his own patients he has found persons whose brain associates music with color or taste and cases where the brain makes music on its own even against the desire of the person. And then there is the strange independence of the two hemispheres of the brain. Sacks points to a patient with an [left brain] IQ of under sixty who can nevertheless comprehend and sing from memory thousands of arias in thirty-five languages!

For a very long time it has been observed that we seem to be two separate people: we have a rational or intellectual side but we also have an experiential side. We learn by reading or by instruction and we learn by experience. Modern clinical research with regard to our two brain hemispheres does seem to indicate that the left hemisphere ('left brain') deals with language, math and rational information. The right hemisphere deals with spatial understanding, emotions and experiential knowledge, including music. It is quite a bit more complex than this, of course. For example it appears that we hear the melody of 'music' in a different part of the brain than time and rhythm. But perhaps that only reflects the fact that time and rhythm are rational data whereas by 'music' most people would mean feeling or emotion. Sacks points, for example, to research done by Isabelle Peretz and colleagues in Montreal.

Dr Oliver Sacks

[1] Oliver Sacks, *Musicophilia* (New York: Knopf, 2007).

> They feel that there are two basic categories of musical perception, one involving the recognition of melodies, the other the perception of rhythm or time intervals. Impairments of melody usually go with right-hemisphere lesions, but representation of rhythm is much more

widespread and robust and involves not only the left hemisphere, but many subcortical systems in the basal ganglia, the cerebellum and other areas.²

[2] Quoted in Sacks, ibid., 109.

We might add there is no surprise that they found melody being perceived in the 'right-brain' for other studies suggest that melody is the chief vehicle for emotions in music.

With this one example we acknowledge the complexity of the brain's organization with respect to music, however, in order to enable us to speak of the generalizations in the perception of music which seem important we will continue to use the terms left- and right-brain, in spite of the fact that these terms are out of fashion in some circles.

The great significance for music education in the clinical research of the past forty or so years is that it demonstrates the unique definition of music itself. It shares nothing important with the rational concepts of the left-brain. And right here one sees how ironic and absurd is the fact that music education has since the 1950s elected to concentrate on the 'concepts' of music rather than on its true essence, the experiential nature of music. Music has its own special characteristics and forms of Truth. Medical science has given music education the greatest possible gift: a way to prove the importance of music to the child and for the curriculum of all children. But during the past forty years the field of music education in general has failed to grasp this great gift.

I have often wondered why music educators lag so far behind other disciplines with respect to basic research. Perhaps music teachers are simply too busy to keep up with their reading—it takes them a decade to catch up. How else can one explain the sudden enthusiasm with behavioral principles in music education during the 1970s, when the field of psychology itself had long since examined, considered, and lost interest in Skinner and his theories? As Psychologist Michael Corballis observed,

> [Since 1964] the influence of behaviorism has waned, and it is no longer the dominant force in psychology.³

[3] Michael C. Corballis, *The Lopsided Ape* (New York: Oxford University Press, 1991), 19.

And so it is again with medicine's discoveries of how the hemispheres of our brain process information, a topic obviously basic to any kind of education. When I first spoke on this subject, in a 1974 keynote address before the Texas Music Educators Convention, I found no music teacher in the audience well-read on this subject and indeed one university music professor declared that I was a lunatic. Now, thirty-seven years later, and after the basic research I spoke of has been awarded the Nobel Prize in Medicine, I find the subject is common knowledge in all circles and among students even at the high school level. But even music educators who have kept up with their reading on clinical brain research seem afraid of this topic. I recall attempting to discuss this with two previous presidents of MENC, both personal friends, who were literally afraid to even discuss the implications of clinical research on music education.

In particular, there seem to be two general findings in clinical research which seem to paralyze music education leaders.

The first of these has been various reports of clinical evidence that some musicians listen to music with the left hemisphere (right ear), whereas 'normal' people listen with the right hemisphere (left ear). In a typical example, two psychologists from Columbia University, Thomas Bever and Robert Chiarello, discovered that when listening to music, musicians tend to use the left brain hemisphere, their analytical side, while those who are 'musically unknowledgeable,' use their right or experiential side.

Some additional research brings this question into clearer focus. First, it has been shown that when musicians trained in traditional European tonal music listen to non-Western music, they too listen with the right hemisphere![4] The real key, I believe, to what we are really talking about here has been found by John Mazziotta, a researcher at UCLA. He found that most people listened to music with the right hemisphere, but that it was when a listener tried to visualize the music *as it might appear on the page* they mainly used the left hemisphere.[5]

The point here is that it is when 'knowledgeable' musicians try to conceptualize as they listen, which is what we teach them in school to do, they will naturally use the left hemisphere more because the notated form of music is indeed a

[4] R. Johnson, J. Bowers, M. Gamble, F. Lyons, T. Presbey, and R. Vetter, 'Ability to Transcribe Music and Ear Superiority for Tone Sequences,' in *Cortex*, 1977, 13, 295-299.

[5] Reported in *The Wall Street Journal*, August 30, 1985.

symbolic, left hemispheric language, just like English. But that is not what we mean when we say the 'language of music,' and that is the wrong way to listen to music.

> Music is perceived in holistic, emotional fashion, not as an explicit, propositional representation of something. It has been described as a 'language' of the right hemisphere, but one that is emotional, nonverbal, and holistic.[6]

In summary, I feel this research finding only confirms that the feeling and emotive nature of music is heard in the right hemisphere and the conceptual details of music are heard in the left hemisphere—which is exactly what we would expect. Other than that, if it has any significance for music education, it is that music education has ruined these particular musicians' ability to 'hear' the most important essence of music. This, therefore prevents the music educator from saying, 'Music is of the Right Hemisphere.' But this is no surprise; rhythm as we teach it has to do with numbers and numbers are left hemisphere. That is why we conductors conduct the meter with the right hand (left hemisphere) and try to show nonverbal, 'musical,' expressive things with the left hand (right hemisphere).[7]

The fact is, music, because music is a language, is found to some degree in *both* hemispheres, and probably for the same reason English is—because the corpus callosum is not fully connected for the first years of life, thereby causing each hemisphere to absorb languages before they began to specialize. The real question is, 'Which hemisphere is most adapted to deal with the language in question?' We know the left hemisphere is best adapted to deal with English. How about music?

Important research with regard to where we hear music began with observation of stroke or brain damaged patients. Maurice Ravel suffered left hemisphere damage at age fifty-seven due to a car wreck, but was still musically skilled in the right hemisphere. Similarly, the Russian composer V. B. Shebalin suffered severe left hemisphere damage at age fifty-one, but continued to compose important works.

Interestingly enough, Tedd Judd, a psychologist at the Pacific Medical Center in Seattle, had a composer–patient who suffered a stroke in the right hemisphere. This patient could still compose simple melodies, but lost the ability to compose

[6] Corballis, op. cit., 268 and D. Falk, 'Hominid paleoneurology,' in *Annual Review of Anthropology*, 1987, 16, 13-30.

[7] Pianos are, of course, built exactly backwards! They should have reversed keyboards, so the left hand can play the expressive melodies and the right hand the plodding rhythms. There were built as they are, centuries before the discoveries of brain research, simply because of the observation that most people are right-handed. They are designed for right-handed players, not right-hemisphere musicians. Radical as this sounds to the pianist reader, may I only appeal that you may be doing everything the hardest possible way. And what about Mozart, who loved to play with his hands crossed. It would not have been the only case in which he *knew* something the rest of us did not!

Maurice Ravel

counterpoint.[8] Elliott Ross, a neurologist at the University of Texas Medical School, found that patients with right hemisphere strokes may speak in monotones—they lose the ability to make their speech 'musical.'[9] These findings relative to stroke patients are summarized by Howard Gardner:

[8] Reported in *The Wall Street Journal*, op. cit.

[9] ibid.

> Studies show that when someone suffers damage to the nervous system through a stroke or tumor, all abilities do not break down equally. If you have an injury to areas of the left hemisphere of the brain, you will lose your language ability almost entirely, but that will not affect your musical, spatial or interpersonal skills to the same extent.
>
> Conversely, you can have lesions in your right hemisphere that leave language capacity intact but that seriously compromise spatial, musical or interpersonal abilities.
>
> So we have a special capacity for language that is unconnected to our capacity for music or interpersonal skills, and vice versa.[10]

[10] Howard Gardner, 'Human Intelligence Isn't What We Think It Is,' *U. S. News & World Report*, March 19, 1984.

In another interesting study, musical ability tests were conducted at the California Institute of Technology by Drs. Joseph Bogen and H. W. Gordon on eight subjects using sodium amylobarbitone, a drug that paralyzes a selected hemisphere for between three and five minutes when injected into the appropriate artery.

> When the right hemisphere was drugged, the subjects were able to sing the lyrics with proper rhythm, but their pitch was either monotonic or off-key, and their intonation was uncontrolled. Speech intonation, oddly, was unaffected, leading to the conclusion that music intonation and language intonation are independent of each other and are located in opposite hemispheres.
>
> When the left hemisphere was drugged, singing was normal (considering the general drowsiness brought on by the drug). Rhythm appeared to be normal no matter which hemisphere was drugged, and, curiously, so did lyrics.
>
> The explanation for this seemingly misplaced verbal ability is something called 'automatic language.' No one really knows exactly how it works, but when we learn something by rote to such an extent that it is lodged permanently in our memory and requires no interpretive or linguistic skills (other than those needed to mouth the words), the knowledge seems to be accessible to both hemispheres. Thus an experienced Shakespearean actor with severe left-hemisphere damage might be able to recite *Hamlet* while being unable to ask the time of day.[11]

[11] Craig Buck, 'Knowing the LEFT from the RIGHT,' *Human Behavior*, June, 1976.

These tests certainly suggest that the right hemisphere is most adept in the perception of music—even the 'details' of music. As a matter of fact, even persons who have the left hemisphere completely removed[12] still retain musical ability, including melody, rhythm, intonation, and associated lyrics in the right hemisphere, proving the right hemispherical nature of musical understanding. By the way, I can not help observing that since music is primarily of the domain of the right hemisphere, and therefore unique to the *individual*, perhaps it is a misnomer to call it 'the International Language'—it is in fact a *personal* language, as we shall emphasize below.

I might also mention that research has shown that the right hemisphere is also superior in the perception of vocal non-speech sounds, such as coughing, laughing and crying.[13]

For me, personal experience has convinced me that the location of musical experience in the brain is clearly separated from language. I have often had the experience, after an intense rehearsal when I was completely absorbed in the music, that a student would come up and ask some simple question—it could be, 'Where is the pencil sharpener?'—and I would find myself unable to answer. I would always understand the question, but it was as if I could not find the language to answer. While this condition might only last a few seconds after rehearsal, I nevertheless had the impression that the left hemisphere had simply been turned off. In light of this experience, I was not surprised to find a letter of Schumann in which he complains of the same problem.

> My thoughts and actions are so absorbed by Art, that I am nearly forgetting German, especially how to make the letters of the alphabet.[14]

[12] ibid.

[13] Doreen Kimura, 'The Asymmetry of the Human Brain,' *Scientific American* (1973), 228.

[14] Letter to Julius Schumann, July 18, 1832.

Interesting Characteristics of Musical Perception in the Brain

Diana Deutsch, who has developed some of the most extraordinary finding regarding musical perception, has discovered some startling facts about how we perceive pitch. First, that our species has a built in 'perfect pitch' template. While she has observed that this has evolved as an association with the pitch used for speaking, the origin no doubt lies with the perception of the natural overtone series by early man.

Second, she has found that we hear high pitches in the right ear, and low pitches in the left ear, even though our brain makes us think we are hearing everything in *both* ears!

> Diana Deutsch of the University of California at San Diego suggests that even though most people can't consciously name a particular note as an F or a B-flat, for instance—an ability known as true perfect pitch—the brain nevertheless categorizes the tones according to a musical scale fixed deep within the mind. In other words, most people possess a subconscious form of 'perfect pitch.'
>
> Even more surprising is Deutsch's discovery that this mental musical template depends on the range of sounds people use for language—and is different for people in different communities. Those who heard the experimental tones as changing the same way also spoke with the same range of sounds in their voices. Furthermore, students at U. C. San Diego perceived the notes as changing in a manner different from the perceptions of groups of people in Sweden and Austria.
>
> ...
>
> Experiments by Deutsch demonstrate that the brain sorts out the noises it hears by grouping together sounds that appear to come from the same direction, and that it accomplishes this by listening for high-pitched notes. Because high notes don't travel as far as low ones—which is why the bass drum of an oncoming marching band can be heard long before the piccolos—the brain assumes that the ear hearing the highest notes is closest to the musical source ... most people hear high-pitched sounds coming through the right ear best ...
>
> Proof that this direction-finding mechanism is but one of many mental 'modules' operating simultaneously to shape the mind's perceptions came when Deutsch made one module override another. Playing alternating high and low tones into a person's left ear and the reverse pattern into the right, Deutsch found that listeners heard all the high notes as if they were coming into the right ear and all the low notes as though they were coming into the left. The rapidly alternating directional cues apparently confused the mental mechanism responsible for detecting direction, causing it to override the module responsible for perceiving the sound itself and to create the musical 'illusion' of each ear's hearing notes that weren't there.[15]

This last finding suggests that orchestras evolved their seating plans with the first violins to the audiences' left because the musicians on stage naturally wanted to hear the melody in

[15] 'The Musical Brain,' *U. S. News & World Report*, June 11, 1990. Deutsch also discovered the curious fact that when presented with pairs of complex tones that were electronically engineered so as not to rise or fall, subjects nevertheless heard some tone pairs as rising and others as descending!

their *right* ear. Therefore, Deutsch has observed the best way for the audience to hear a symphony orchestra would be for the audience to be suspended from the ceiling by their feet!

Another curious, and very important, characteristic of our perception of music—which may also date back to the pre-speech vowel based 'musical communication' of early man—is that we have a biological affinity for *melodic patterns*.

Research by Dr. Jamshed Bharucha, of Dartmouth College, with 'non-musicians' demonstrated that when the brain network

> was given the first few notes of a particular melody and then asked to predict the note to follow, the brain model's first reaction was to produce the most expected note based on the general musical pattern it had learned. Only after that general rule failed did it produce the note it had learned by rote.
>
> The experiment suggests that the enjoyment of familiar music may have roots in the brain's extraordinary ability to draw on its vast store of implicit knowledge about general patterns: Listening to a familiar piece, the brain not only remembers the exact note that is to come but, more important, also knows how closely the note fits within the more general pattern of expectations it has learned over the years.[16]

[16] 'The Musical Brain,' op. cit.

This revelation that our brain has a fondness for familiar patterns helps answer Aristotle's question, 'Why do we prefer music we already know?'[17] We know this to be the case, even though one would assume that musicians, especially, would always find new music more interesting, as we are always interested in the newest car, the newest food, etc.

[17] *Problemata*, XIX, 5.

This also helps explain why composers and other musically astute persons often err in their evaluation of other contemporary composers. Some examples:

> 'Beethoven lacked a sense of beauty' [Ludwig Spohr, on hearing Beethoven's Ninth Symphony for the first time.]

> 'A complete lack of order and color. This music is hideous. Such a perversion of euphony, such a rape of the beautiful should have been punished by law. Such music should come under police jurisdiction.' [The poet, Grillparzer, on hearing Weber's *Euryanthe*.]

> 'Now that I've worked my way through Brahms, I've fallen back on Bruckner again. What an odd pair of second-raters ... All I can say of Brahms is that he's a puny little dwarf.' [Mahler, in a letter to his wife.]

This biological affinity for musical patterns is present in the brains of other species as well. A recent study by Stewart Hulse of Johns Hopkins University found that starlings have the ability to recognize a simple melody in different keys, and other studies suggest that dolphins recognize octaves. In another experiment, pigeons were trained to distinguish random excerpts of music by J. S. Bach from excerpts by Igor Stravinsky, and they were even able to correctly categorize music by other composers as being either 'Bach-like' or 'Stravinsky-like'.[18]

Jay Dowling, of the University of Texas at Dallas, has discovered clinical evidence to suggest that ordinary people perceive these melodic patterns on the basis of the relationship between the notes themselves, and not on the basis of precise pitches. Thus, almost everybody can sing 'Happy Birthday' starting from any note on the piano.[19]

Diana Deutsh has documented the extraordinary degree to which our brain deals with melodic patterns.

> The brain's quest to find overall patterns in the seemingly random world is evident in experiments by Deutsch that show that the mind will rearrange a jumble of notes it hears into familiar patterns. Playing a complex array of notes in one ear and a different complex musical pattern in the other, Deutsch discovered that her subjects in fact heard two simple musical passages. Faced with a barrage of confusing sounds, the brains of Deutsch's subjects simply combined the notes that were closest to each other into familiar tunes. This same effect occurs as the brain weaves together the myriad notes played simultaneously by an orchestra in a performance: in Tchaikowsky's Sixth Symphony, for example, the violins, viola and cello each play musical passages that actually are never heard by most people in the audience because the brain automatically rearranges the combined notes of these instruments into different—and more familiar—musical patterns.
>
> The brain's effort to tease out general patterns often takes place without a person even being aware of it.[20]

Thus we have yet another example of one of our 'other minds' at work!

[18] 'The Musical Brain,' op. cit.

[19] ibid.

[20] ibid.

24 Music Education of the Future

On the other hand, the brain's natural biological affinity for logical melodic patterns does not mean that we are equipped by nature to recognize such patterns when presented backwards.

> Not all of the public's bewilderment about modern music can be attributed to lack of familiarity, however; in fact, it may be due to the biological limitations of the brain. Some modern composers, for instance, build structure into their music by inverting a melody or playing its notes in reverse order. Despite the brain's wizardry in picking out many kinds of overall structure in a mass of details, these kinds of patterns are hard for the brain to recognize, notes Stanford University's John Pierce, author of *The Science of Musical Sound*. For example, most people don't realize that the sound of the word *we* is the reverse of the sound of *you*.[21]

[21] ibid.

This fact, of course, contradicts one of the basic premises of 12-tone music—that everyone is supposed to be able to hear the row backwards, etc. I am reminded of an account of a party in Leonard Bernstein's apartment in New York City, when this was the subject of the conversation. Everyone said, 'Of course I can hear all the versions of the row in Schoenberg's *Moses and Aaron*.' Bernstein reportedly went to a piano and played 'The Star Spangled Banner' backwards and no one could identify it!

Leonard Bernstein, 1971

Another characteristic of the mind which is extremely important to our enjoyment of music is a preference of the brain to choose generalization over precision. The origin of this is adaptation and as a result we don't have to discriminate a specific car horn in order to jump out of the way—any car horn will do. This characteristic has some very valuable benefits for us, both in music and in our daily life.

> The interaction of these various modules of the mind may be responsible for the brain's ability to be precise and to generalize at the same time. The ears can perceive sounds as low as a rumbling subway car and as high as a bird's chirp and distinguish the minuscule differences in notes produced by twisting the tuning knob of a violin ever so slightly. Yet studies of music from around the world suggest that despite the ear's ability to make minute discriminations of sounds, most cultures divide the vast range of audible sounds into musical scales of only about five to seven notes. That the brain is willing to sacrifice some precision and allow a single note to represent a broad range of sounds is evident in opera where a singer's vibrato moves the sound of the note up and

down quickly but never stays long on the exact pitch. Yet the singer is perceived as being on key. As with many mental processes involved in music, the brain's willingness to trade precision for generalization may help people adapt in other arenas: It explains, for example, why people can understand a person's speech even though it is heavily accented or recognize the aged face of a long-lost acquaintance.[22]

[22] ibid.

The most important benefit of this for us as music listeners is that it spares us the burden of listening to details in music, which would deprive us of the more important communication of feeling. For example, it would be terrible if, in listening to Beethoven's Third Symphony, or Mahler's Ninth Symphony, if we were continually distracted by thoughts such as, 'Oh! there's a second inversion subdominant chord!' If this were not the case, we would all be like the three blind men in the famous Sufi story who encountered an elephant. One, holding the tail, observed, 'An elephant is similar to a buggy whip.' The second blind man, feeling a leg, said, 'An elephant is like a great column of a building.' The third man, holding the trunk, thought the elephant to be a large member of the snake family. They all knew the *details* of the elephant, but none knew the *elephant*.

This is the key to one of the most important characteristics of our perception of music, the process by which we understand emotion in music. It works like this. When an orchestra performs a piece of music which we might call generally 'sad,' shall we say Tchaikovsky's Sixth Symphony, what travels through space and communicates to the listener is not a specific form of sadness, but a quintessence of the emotion, the essence of the emotion in its purest and most concentrated form. We don't even *want* to know the specific source of sadness when a composer writes a 'sad' composition—which may have been that his cat died, or something.

Then the remarkable thing happens. Each listener in the concert hall takes in this quintessence of sadness through his senses (in this case, his ears), and sifts this form of the emotion through the experiential data-bank of his right hemisphere, where this emotion (and this music) takes on a personal definition when it interfaces with that listener's own personal understanding of that emotion. In this way we hear music both generally and personally. Each of two thousand members of the audience hears a different Tchaikovsky Sixth Symphony—one that communicates directly with their own personal experience.

Wagner called this quintessence of the emotion the *Melos* of the composition, by which he means what I have described.

> What Music expresses is eternal, infinite and ideal; she expresses not the passion, love, desire, of this or that individual in this or that condition, but Passion, Love, Desire itself.[23]

[23] Quoted in William Ashton Ellis, ed., *Wagner's Prose Works* (New York: Boude), VII, 81.

I have the feeling that musical memory, upon which we all so depend, is somehow closely related to this tendency by the brain toward the general, and not the specific. I don't believe any pianist could actively, consciously be aware of each note in a Beethoven Sonata *while* performing it. Ornstein coins the word, 'chunking,' for what he believes describes the generalized memory process.

> When something is organized, it is simplified. The experience of many different 'dots' on a page is quite complex, but a dalmatian near a tree is organized and simple. Because of the vast amount of information in the world, it is important that we simplify it so that we can act quickly.
>
> …
>
> Perhaps there is no sign of a 'storage area' existing in the brain. The neural connections are like an enormous network of interconnected wires, but nowhere do they terminate in one location as one would expect if there were a memory file in the brain. Memories aren't photographic; they do not store individual events; rather, they can be lumped together, erased, or altered by later experiences.
>
> We remember the semblance, not the signals. As our minds adapt to fit our changing situations and needs, so our perceptions and memories change as well. If we are very hungry, a shopping center nearby is recalled as a source of food, rather than as a place to idle away time looking at clothes. Once our hunger is sated, we may then remember that we wanted to check out a sale at one of the boutiques.
>
> The hard points in the brain select basic signals from the world, colors, edges, and corners. The ability to organize information, to be creative, to be competent, even to remember, is the ability to link these 'fragments,' using the maps that seem to exist inside the nervous system.
>
> A unit of memory is called a *chunk*. In perceiving and remembering bits of information, chunking is the process of using a code to organize individual items into units of memory. GEAIMNN is a sequence of seven bits that you can probably retain only briefly. MEANING is a

sequence of the same seven bits, but you have a code (in this case, the English language) that can organize them into a chunk (in this case, the word *meaning*).

The mind continually processes the world, and what is a semblance one time may eventually chunk into a signal. To a child letters were once distinct, but we don't have any idea how many e's there are on a page or how many pages we have read. 'What's in that book?' someone asks. 'Nothing,' you say, consigning thousands of letters, millions of dots of ink, recipes, racetrack and stock reports, quiet diplomacy, sewer bursts, to oblivion.

The ability to chunk information greatly expands the storage capacity of memory because small signals combine into larger chunks that are then more easily remembered. Knowing a code increases the capacity of memory and the ability to remember …

Chunking allows us to recall a large amount of information, in other words, to build up complex semblances based on subtle signals from the world. With feature detectors in perception, we saw how a prewired capacity to see small elements such as line ends or vertices could lead to the ability to discriminate classes of objects. In memory, whole events, era, or abstract concepts are tied to simple perceptions or symbols …

Chunks of memory linked together build up, step by step. Each time a link is repeated, it is strengthened, and the neural organization behind it becomes more fixed, less flexible.[24]

[24] Robert Ornstein, *The Evolution of Consciousness* (New York: Prentice Hall, 1991), 177, 184ff.

Ornstein also discusses the brain's tendency to then *overemphasize* that which it has first understood by generalization. This is related to something common to all musicians, the fact that we perceive music in a somewhat distorted fashion. A familiar example is the fact that we 'hear' higher tones louder than lower tones, therefore conductors must balance in reverse just to make us think we are hearing the music in the apparent balance of the score page.

Adaptation is doing the best job in any circumstances, be it selecting the quicker of two routes, identifying the greatest threat, picking the ripest fruit, or finding the safest place to sleep. This ancestral system of simpletons (what I've called the SOB) is what makes us such avid and dazed shoppers today. Shifting the mind in place is the job of advertisers, who shift adaptation, attention, and more to get us to do what they want …

Prior judgments anchor future ones because they shift our simpletons around … you may notice the change if you are accustomed to carrying a 2-pound briefcase home from the office, and suddenly your workload sends you home with a 3-pound one. However, if you are hauling wood, you will be very unlikely to notice the difference between a 50- and a 51-pound load.

Of course, these errors are rare and are instances of the ability to simplify the world. The ability to generalize saves effort. We need not waste time discriminating the sound of one car horn from another to get out of the way; different-sounding telephone rings all signal the same thing. Moreover, we are conscious of only a few things at once.

Since the mind evolved to select a few signals and then dream up a semblance, *whatever enters our consciousness is overemphasized*. It does not matter how the information enters, whether via a television program, a newspaper story, a friend's conversation, a strong emotional reaction, a memory—all is overemphasized. We ignore other, more compelling evidence, overemphasizing and overgeneralizing from the information close at hand to produce a rough-and-ready reality.[25]

We look forward to medical science discovering more about how we perceive music physically. But we already know the most important thing: Music is the right hemisphere equivalent of the left hemisphere's English. It is Music which speaks for the experiential side of us, as English speaks for the data side of us.

That is an argument of great significance for music education if the goal of education is to educate the whole child![26]

[25] ibid., 256.

[26] As, for example, George P. Moore, of the University of Southern California, has found that most people can not walk and chew gum at different tempi, because the brain can apparently only monitor one internal metronome at a time! (*Wall Street Journal*, op. cit.)

3   *Purpose and Meaning in Music Education*

THE EXTANT WRITINGS OF THE ANCIENT GREEKS document that civilization had concluded by some even earlier time that the paramount purpose of music is to communicate emotions, as we see already in the oldest literature of Western Europe, where Homer describes Ulysses crying as a minstrel sings. Plato, in *Ion*,[1] presents a valuable discussion between Socrates and a Rhapsodist, the ancient singer of epic poetry, during which the singer describes the emotions of the audience while he sings.

[1] 534c–535e.

> ION. I look down upon them from the stage, and behold the various emotions of pity, wonder, sternness, stamped upon their faces when I am performing.

Plato, in fact, defined music as, 'a science of the phenomena of love in its application to harmony and rhythm.'[2]

[2] Plato, *Symposium*, 187b.

The ancient writers also clearly recognized the fact that the ability to appreciate and understand music is not dependent on any technical knowledge whatsoever. In other words, the teaching of concepts contributes nothing in educating the person for hearing and appreciating music. The teaching of concepts in music only educates the individual to understand those concepts—things *about* music, but not *music* itself.

Petrarch, for example, quotes Cicero as saying the music 'tickles their ears, without their knowing why.'[3] It is remarkable that an almost identical statement was made by Mozart in a letter to his father.

[3] Letter to Boccaccio, in James Robinson, *Petrarch, The First Modern Scholar and Man of Letters* (New York: Putnam, 1914), 184.

> These passages are written in such a way that the less learned cannot fail to be pleased, though without knowing why.[4]

[4] 28 December 1782.

With the beginning of the Christian Era, the construction of concert halls, private and public concerts of art music, together with popular music and sung poetry, all continued, although one would never discover this in reading music history texts which describe the Middle Ages. There was, however, a new development which had far reaching consequences in music practice. The new Christian Church, consumed with the desire to rid Western Europe of all things 'pagan' (meaning the values, books and music of ancient Greece and Rome), took a very strong stand against all expression of emotions. Emotions, the Church fathers proclaimed, were the path to sin. St. Basil even proposed that the proper Christian should not even laugh because laughing is a form of emotion. This, no doubt, is why nowhere in the fourth-century New Testament is Jesus described as laughing. After the Fall of Rome, the new Church attacked art in general, reasoning that the Christian should not love art—for to love art is to love the present life, which is inconsistent with believing in, and living for, the promised future life.[5]

The Church rather grudgingly accepted vocal music, as indeed it had to because of the legend of the choir of angels singing at the time of the birth of Jesus and the reference in the New Testament to Jesus singing.[6] Reflecting their prejudice, the Church stressed that in church singing it is the words that matter, not the music. Augustine wrote that whenever he found himself listening to the music, instead of thinking about the words, he felt he had sinned.[7] Regarding the music itself there was the additional problem that it 'disappeared' when the performance ended, as mentioned by the third-century Church philosopher, Lactantius.

> For all those things which are unconnected with words, that is, pleasant sounds of the air and of strings, may be easily disregarded, because they do not adhere to us, and cannot be written [notated].[8]

For its schools, the early Church could therefore only admit the study of music when it was presented in conceptual terms, and, in particular, as mathematics. The influential Boethius (475–524 AD), although he acknowledges in passing the power of the emotional aspect in music by noting 'that we cannot be free from it even if we so desired,'[9] he nevertheless clearly sought to establish the principle that it is not enough for a musician to know *music*, he must know *about* music. From this judgment, his conclusion followed:

> How much nobler, then, is the study of music as a rational discipline than as composition and performance![10]

[5] St. John Chrysostom, 'Commentary on Saint John,' trans., Sister Thomas Aquinas Goggin (New York: Fathers of the Church, 1960), 227.

[6] Together with his disciples in Matthew 26:30.

[7] *The Confessions*, X.

[8] Lactantius, 'The Divine Institutes,' trans., William Fletcher in *The Works of Lactantius* (Edinburgh: T. & T. Clark, 1886), I, Book VI, xxi.

[9] Boethius, *Fundamentals of Music*, trans., Calvin Bower (New Haven: Yale University Press), I, i.

[10] ibid., I, xxxiv. Fifteen centuries later our music schools still labor under these misconceptions.

From this nonsense, Church philosophers established the definition of 'musician' to be not one who makes music, but one who *knows about* music. The mere performer was given a much lower social status, thus Aurelian of Réome, in his *Musica Disciplina* (ca. 843 AD), could observe, 'The singer seems to stand before the musician like a prisoner before the judge.'[11] John Cotton, in his music treatise of 1100 AD, says the musician who doesn't *know about* music is a beast by definition.[12]

There must have been many who regarded this official thinking as the nonsense that it is. One was the tenth-century nun, Hrotswitha, who has left a play, *Paphnutius*, which contains an extensive dialog on the subject of music.[13] The passage begins with a group of students asking the teacher, 'What *is* music?' The teacher responds with various mathematical complexities based on Boethius, each one of which causes the students to object to this conceptual language and respond, 'What has this got to do with *music*?,' implying, we presume, that they understood that music has to do with feelings and emotions, not mathematics. The teacher answers in frustration, 'But that is how you *talk* about music!'

When the first Church universities began to be established, music was placed in the faculty of mathematics and all music courses were taught by, and music treatises written by, mathematicians. But these professors were very much aware that the actual performance of music which they *heard* included fundamental elements, such as feeling, which were not easily represented or explained by numbers, or any other conceptual symbols. Hence they simply separated the discipline of music at this time into two branches: *musica speculativa* and *musica practica*. They said, in effect, 'We will teach the first, and leave to you players the second.'

Thus we have inherited two forms of music, a *speculativa* form, which includes notation and all of 'theory' which we can talk and write about, and which we learn by eye, and a *practica* form which is mostly learned by ear (the private studio teacher says, 'No, it goes like this'). But in truth, the *speculativa* form does not exist. It is only a conceptual symbolic language which only *represents* the *practica* form, which is *real* music! Thus, when music schools teach the conceptual form, while they

[11] Aurelian of Réome, *The Discipline of Music*, trans., Joseph Ponte (Colorado Springs: Colorado College Music Press, 1968), VII.

[12] John gives the source as the 'Micrologus,' but it actually comes from the beginning of Guido's 'Regulae rhythmicae.'

[13] *The Plays of Hrotswitha of Gandersheim,* trans., Larissa Bonfante (New York: New York University Press, 1979), 108ff.

call it music, they are not really teaching music. Harmony, for example, is not music and might better be identified as another symbolic language.

These views of music are still found as late as the famous Johannes Tinctoris (1435–1511), who identified himself as one who professes 'the mathematical sciences.'[14] It is particularly interesting that after the publication of his mathematics-based book on proportions, *Proportionale Musices*, he was criticized by a singer, a 'practical' musician. Indeed, Tinctoris confides this man 'has not been afraid to menace me with a violent meal of this little book if ever I should return to my native land.'

It was only the rediscovery and publication of the ancient Greek treatises which finally led to the rejection of the old Church nonsense about music and restored an understanding of the true nature of music. It was this Renaissance movement which we call Humanism in music. We can clearly see a change is in the air in the first decade of the fourteenth century, in the writings of Marchetto of Padua. In considering the etymology of the word 'voice' [*vox*] he notes that it comes from 'vows' [*vota*], 'because it expresses vows of the heart.' He then quotes Aristotle as saying of the spoken voice, 'Things spoken are symbols of the passions of the soul.'[15] He concludes it is appropriate, therefore, that we speak of 'notes' of music, which derives from *nota* ('symbol'). He means that the notes are not the *real* music, but only symbols of the real music.

As the Renaissance began to release common sense from the chains of the Church's artificial definitions of music, one finds poets gaining the courage to satirize the old phony ideas of the Church. In Petrarch we find a passage in which 'Joy' and 'Reason' are clearly representatives of Humanism and the Church.

> JOY: Song moves me.
> REASON: But to what purpose? Without doubt music has great power over the noble hearts of men. But its effects are various beyond belief. And, to omit what is of no concern [to the Church], it moves some to shallow mirth, others to pure and devout joy and, sometimes, even to pious tears.[16]

[14] *Concerning the Nature and Propriety of Tones*, trans., Albert Seay (Colorado Springs, 1976), 1.

[15] Marchetto of Padua, *Lucidarium*, Jan W. Herlinger, trans., (Chicago: University of Chicago Press, 1985), I, 10, iiiff.

[16] 'Remedies for Fortune Fair and Foul,' trans., Conrad Rawski (Bloomington: Indiana University Press, 1991), I, xxiii, 71.

An especially interesting reference to the importance of *feeling* in music is found in Chaucer's 'Nun's Priest's Tale.' A fox who has come to hear a rooster sing, declares that the rooster sings with more feeling in his music than Boethius or any other Church singer.

> Therwith ye han in musyk moore feelynge
> Than hadde Boece, or any that kan synge.[17]

[17] 'Nun's Priest's Tale,' 4483

By the fifteenth century Humanism had made the emotions a topic of general discussion. The Florentine philosopher, Leon Battista Alberti (b. 1404), gives an interesting testimonial to the power of love and, more significantly, points out that it is only by *experience* that one can understand such an emotion.

> Who would believe, except by the experience of his own feelings, how great and intense is the love of a father toward his children? Every kind of love seems to me no small matter. Many have been known to risk all their possessions, to give time and fortune, to undergo terrible hardships, dangers, and troubles only to display their loyalty and the quality of their love for a friend. And it is said that there have been men who, for desire of things loved which they thought they had lost, refused to continue living.[18]

[18] Leon Battista Alberti, *I Libri dela Famiglia*, trans., Renée Watkins (Columbia: University of South Carolina Press, 1969), I, 45.

And at this time Leonardo da Vinci observed,

> The tears come from the heart and not from the brain.[19]

[19] Quoted in Jean Paul Richter, ed., *The Literary Works of Leonardo da Vinci* (London: Phaidon, 1970), II, 93. Found together with notes on anatomy!

By the sixteenth century the paramount purpose of music had been restored to what it had been understood to be by the ancient Greeks. Galilei wrote in 1581, 'True music has a primary purpose to express the passions' and, secondarily, 'to communicate these with equal force to the minds of mortals for their benefit and advantage.'[20] Certainly in no medieval music treatise does one find a statement such as this one by Martin Luther: 'Only music deserves being extolled as the mistress and governess of the feelings of the human heart.'[21] Galilei's book on lute intabulation, by the way, gives an almost startling description of the emotions capable on the lute. No organist, he observes, can produce

[20] Oliver Strunk, *Source Readings in Music History* (New York: Norton, 1950), 306ff.

[21] Luther, Preface to a collection of part-songs (1538) based on the suffering and death of Jesus.

> the cries, laments, shrieks, tears, and finally quietude and rage—with so much grace and skill as excellent players do on the lute.[22]

[22] Vincenzo Galilei, *Fronimo* (1584), trans., Carol MacClintock (Neuhasen-Stuttgart: Hänssler-Verlag, 1985), 87.

The university treatises of the Renaissance still speak of music as being mathematics, but finally one is quite different. The *Compendium Musices* by Adrian Coclico (ca. 1550–1562) documents the beginning of a shift away from the old Scholastic complexities of speculative music to the more modern emphasis on expressive, practical musicianship.[23] In this work, written for the training of boy singers, he constantly warns against rules-based learning. No sooner has he begun writing of scales, for example, than he stops and observes that this can only be understood in performance.

[23] Adrian Coclico, *Musical Compendium*, trans., Albert Seay (Colorado Springs: Colorado College Music Press, 1973), 30.

> I have wished to train this boyish industry in music through but few words and precepts on that account, so that no youth running to the books of musician-mathematicians will waste his life in reading them and never arrive at the goal of singing well.[24]

[24] ibid., 10.

Of all the periods of music history, none has been more inaccurately portrayed by musicologists than the Renaissance. Music history texts give the impression that Church music *was* Renaissance music, whereas in fact there was a great deal more than that. A composer such as Machaut would have been utterly astonished if he could have known that he would be remembered today for his Church music, an insignificant proportion of his music and music upon which he placed little value in comparison to his love songs. It is also because music history texts concentrate only on Church music that we never read that the people who actually knew Leonardo da Vinci considered him the greatest *musician* they knew. And why have these same books kept from us such powerful descriptions of performances of art music as that by Francesco da Milano in 1555?

> He made the very strings to swoon beneath his fingers and transported all who listened into such gentle melancholy that one present buried his head in his hands, another let his entire body slump into an ungainly posture with members all awry, while another, his mouth sagged open and his eyes more than half shut, seemed, one would judge, as if transfixed upon the strings, and yet another, with chin sunk upon his chest, hiding the most sadly taciturn visage ever seen, remained abstracted in all his senses save his hearing, as if his soul had fled from all the seats of sensibility to take refuge in his ears where more easefully it could rejoice in such enchanting symphony.[25]

[25] Pontus de Tyard, *Solitaire second* (1555).

Who has ever read a description of listeners of Renaissance Church music which compares with that? The truth of the matter is that the Church polyphony, upon which our modern music history texts are based, was music heard by the actual people living during the Renaissance as being already old-fashioned and scholastic. This was because this music was composed upon principles of mathematics, and not of feeling. For example, Pontus de Tyard, a member of the group of French poets known as the Pléiade, observed,

> Contrapuntal music most often brings to the ears only a lot of noise, from which you feel no vivid effect.[26]

[26] Pontus de Tyard, *Les Discours philosophiques* (Paris, 1587).

Similarly, Zarlino wrote,

> At times nothing is heard but a jumbled din of voices and diverse instrumental sounds, singing without taste or discretion, and an unseemly pronunciation of words, so that he hears only a tumult and uproar. Music practiced in this way cannot have any effect on us worth remembering.[27]

[27] *Le Istitutioni harmoniche*, II, ix, 75.

[28] Quoted in Nino Pirrotta and Elena Povoledo, *Music and Theatre from Poliziano to Monteverdi* (Cambridge: Cambridge University Press, 1982), 241.

It was in the Renaissance, then, that Europe began to rediscover the fundamental role of the emotions in music. The story of the Baroque is one of an obsession for emotions in music by both composers and philosophers alike. Again, the view of the Baroque given us by musicologists over the past one hundred years is so incomplete, and therefore misleading, that many musicians today do not even think of baroque music as being emotional at heart. Many musicians have been misled by their teachers into thinking of baroque music as math, now called counterpoint and functional-bass chord progressions.

[29] *Le Nuove Musiche*, 45.

Caccini, 'Le Nuove Musiche'

But the better baroque composers never talked like that! Cavalieri, in the preface to his *La rappresentatione di Anima* (1600), says his goal is to 'move listeners to different emotions, such as pity and joy, tears and laughter.'[28] And Caccini, in his *Le Nuove Musiche*, writes that the goal of his solo songs was 'to move the affect of the soul.'[29] Charles Butler wrote, in 1636,

> [Good composing is impossible] unless the Author, at the time of Composing, be transported as it were with some Musical fury; so that himself scarce knoweth what he doth, nor can presently give a reason for his doing.[30]

[30] Charles Butler, *The Principles of Musik in Singing and Setting* [1636] (New York: Da Capo Press, 1970), 92.

Angelo Berardi wrote in 1681 that 'Music is the ruler of the passions of the soul.'[31] Speaking of his *Il Gran Tamerlano* (1706), Scarlatti relates that he tried to achieve, 'naturalness and beauty, together with the expression of the passion.'[32] And Karl Philipp Emanuel Bach wrote,

> It appears to me that it is the special province of music to move the heart.[33]

We might also add that in his biographical work, *Ehrenpforte* (Hamburg, 1740), in reference to a person who had claimed both a goal of making 'music a scientific or scholarly pursuit' and an association with J. S. Bach, Johann Mattheson objects that Bach certainly did not teach this man 'the supposed mathematical basis of composition.' 'This,' Mattheson testifies, 'I can guarantee.'[34]

It is at this time also that we find philosophers focusing on the emotions when writing of the purpose of music. Even that left-brained, mechanically obsessed, Descartes, in his definition of music, had to admit,

> The basis of music is sound; its aim is to please and to arouse various emotions in us.[35]

But the real evidence for the consuming interest in the emotions among baroque musicians is found in the contemporary descriptions of their performance. To begin with singers, Severo Bonini has left this description of the singing of one of the first opera composers.

> A much learned singer and composer was Signor Jacopo Peri, who would have moved and brought to tears the hardest heart by singing his works.[36]

And consider the range of emotions mentioned by Christoph Bernhard, in his singing treatise of 1649.

> In the recitative style, one should take care that the voice is raised in moments of anger, and to the contrary dropped in moments of grief. Pain makes it pause; impatience hastens it. Happiness enlivens it. Desire emboldens it. Love renders it alert. Bashfulness holds it back. Hope

[31] Angelo Berardi, *Ragionamenti Musicali* (Bologna, 1681), 87.

[32] Quoted in Claude Palisca, *Baroque Music* (Englewood Cliffs: Prentice Hall, 1981), 236ff.

[33] Quoted in Nat Shapiro, *An Encyclopedia of Quotations About Music* (New York: Da Capo, 1978), 192.

[34] Quoted in Hans T. David and Arthur Mendel, *The Bach Reader* (New York: Norton, 1966), 440.

[35] 'Compendium of Music,' Walter Robert, trans. (American Institute of Musicology, 1961), 11.

[36] Quoted in Nino Pirrotta and Elena Povoledo, op. cit., 246.

strengthens it. Despair diminishes it. Fear keeps it down. Danger is fled with screams. If, however, a person faces up to danger, then his voice must reflect his daring and bravery.[37]

[37] Quoted in Ellen Harris, 'Voices,' in *Performance Practice: Music after 1600* (New York: Norton, 1989), 110.

A manuscript by Diderot describes the nephew of Rameau as an amateur singing in a cafe.

> While singing fragments of Jomelli's *Lamentations*, he reproduced with incredible precision, fidelity, and warmth the most beautiful passages of each scene. In that magnificent recitative in which Jeremiah describes the desolation of Jerusalem he was drenched in tears, which drew their like from every onlooker. His art was complete—delicacy of voice, expressive strength, true sorrow …
>
> Worn out, exhausted, like a man emerging from a deep sleep or a prolonged reverie, he stood motionless, dumb, petrified. He kept looking around him like a man who has lost his way and wants to know where he is. He waited for returning strength and wits, wiping his face with an absent-minded gesture.[38]

[38] Quoted in *Rameau's Nephew and Other Works*, trans., Jacques Barzun (Garden City: Doubleday, 1956), 69.

The most dramatic descriptions of baroque performers are those of violinists, such as this one heard by a French critic in 1702, as

> an ecstatic who was so carried away with the piece that he was playing that he not only martyred his instrument but also himself. No longer master of his own being, he became so transported that he gyrated and hopped around like someone overcome by a demon.[39]

[39] Quoted in Hans-Peter Schmitz, *Die Kunst der Verzierung im 18. Jahrhundert* (Kassel: Bärenreiter, 1955), 12.

The critic, François Raguenet, describes another.

> The artist himself, whilst he is performing it, is seized with an unavoidable agony; he tortures his violin; he racks his body; he is no longer master of himself, but is agitated like one possessed with an irresistible motion.[40]

[40] François Raguenet, 'Parallèle des Italiens et des Français,' (1702), quoted in Strunk, op. cit., 478ff.

If there is still a reader anywhere who is under the impression that baroque music was mechanical and boring, perhaps this eyewitness description of the famous Corelli will make him begin to wonder if he has been previously misinformed.

> I never met with any man that suffered his passions to hurry him away so much whilst he was playing on the violin as the famous Arcangelo Corelli, whose eyes will sometimes turn as red as fire; his countenance will be distorted, his eyeballs roll as in an agony, and he gives in so much to what he is doing that he doth not look like the same man.[41]

[41] O. Strunk, 'François Raguenet, *Comparison between the French and Italian Music* (1702),' in The Musical Quarterly XXXII (1946), 419fn.

In some cases, accounts by contemporary listeners suggest an emotional impact much greater than we might experience in hearing the same music today. The English actor, Betterton, found,

> Purcell penetrates the heart, makes the blood dance through your veins, and thrill with the agreeable violence offered by his Heavenly Harmony.[42]

[42] Charles Gildon, *The Life of Mr. Thomas Betterton, the Late Eminent Tragedian* [1710] (London: Frank Cass Reprint, 1970), 155ff.

And consider the impact of mere incidental music in a play, as recalled by Pepys, in a 27 February 1668 entry in his famous *Diary*.

> What did please me beyond anything in the whole world was the wind-musique when the Angel comes down, which is so sweet that it ravished me; and indeed, in a word, did wrap up my soul so that it make me really sick, just as I have formerly been when in love with my wife; that neither then, nor all the evening going home and at home, I was able to think of anything, but remained all night transported, so as I could not believe that ever any music has that real command over the soul of a man as this did upon me; and makes me resolve to practice wind-music and to make my wife do the same.

One vivid portrait of an attentive audience is found in a description of a performance of Handel.

> The audience was so enchanted with this performance, that a stranger who should have seen the manner in which they were affected, would have imagined they had all been distracted.[43]

[43] J. Mainwaring, *Memoirs of Handel* (1760), quoted in Robert Donnington, *The Interpretation of Early Music* (New York, 1964), 96.

Finally, there is this rather remarkable advice to the listener by Rameau, himself famous during his lifetime as a theoretician.

> Often we think we hear in music only what exists in the words, or in the interpretation we wish to give them. We try to subject music to forced inflections, but that is not the way to be able to judge it. On the contrary, we must not think but let ourselves be carried away by the feeling which the music inspires; without our thinking at all, this feeling will become the basis of our judgment.[44]

[44] Jean Philippe Rameau, *Observations sur notre instinct pour la musique et sur son principe*.

The strong focus on the emotions demonstrated in Italian opera helped prepare the melodically expressive music of the Classic Period. Equally significant was the influence of the Enlightenment which encouraged even the Catholic composers to write music which expressed their own feelings, instead of thinking of themselves as surrogates for God. Now, in expressing emotions, the composers no longer sought the exaggeration of the Baroque, and Italian opera in particular, but instead sought to express more natural and true emotions. Thus, Mozart, describing his *Die Entführung aus dem Serail* for his father, wrote,

> Now, as for Belmonte's aria in A major, do you know how it is expressed—even the throbbing of his loving heart is indicated—the two violins in octaves ... One sees the trembling—the wavering—one sees how his swelling breast heaves—this is expressed by a crescendo—one hears the whispering and the sighing—which is expressed by the first violins, muted, and a flute in unison. Nothing could be more definite than that.[45]

And it is no surprise to find Mozart complimenting Mlle. Weber's singing, by remarking that her singing 'goes to the heart.'[46]

From this time until the twentieth century, no one questioned the fact that the paramount role of music was to express the emotions to the listener. When Beethoven finished his *Missa Solemnis*, he wrote on the score, 'From the heart, may it go to the heart.' Subsequent composers clearly made the expression of emotions through music their credo. Consider the following:

Schumann:
Music is to me the perfect expression of the soul.[47]

Berlioz:
The prevailing characteristics of my music are passionate expression, intense ardor, rhythmical animation, and unexpected turns.[48]

Chopin:
A long time ago I decided that my universe will be the soul and heart of man.[49]

[45] Letter to his father, September 26, 1781.

[46] Letter to his father, February 19, 1778.

[47] Letter to his mother, Leipzig, May 8, 1832.

[48] *Memoirs*.

[49] Letter to Delphine Potocka. Chopin's last words were reported to be, 'Play Mozart in memory of me.'

Verdi:
: I should compose with utter confidence a subject that set my blood going, even though it were condemned by all other artists as anti-musical.[50]

Mahler:
: What is best in music is not to be found in the notes.[51]

Paul Dukas:
: Be it laughter or tears, feverish passion or religious ecstasy, nothing, in the category of human feelings, is a stranger to music.[52]

Max Reger:
: Music, in and by itself, should generate a flow of pure emotion without the least tinge of extraneous rationalization.[53]

Ravel:
: Music, I feel, must be emotional first and intellectual second.[54]

Frederick Delius:
: Music is an outburst of the soul.[55]

Because it was so evident that the purpose of music is to communicate emotion, over a long period of time some philosophers had been speaking of music as an actual language of the emotions. Already in the sixteenth century, Martin Luther had observed, 'Music is a language of feelings without words.'[56] Subsequent philosophers in France, Descartes, Chénier, Nodier, Chabanon, De Vismes and J.-J. Rousseau in particular, began to speculate on the possibility of an international language based on music which might replace traditional languages. The extraordinary attempts of Jean-François Sudre to realize this dream with his *Langue Musicale Universelle* had no successor, with the exception of Wagner, who almost certainly found his leitmotif idea here.

Some other familiar persons commented on the role of music as a language, among them:

Mendelssohn:
: People usually complain that music is so ambiguous; that it is so doubtful what they ought to think when they hear it; whereas everyone understands words. With me it is entirely the reverse. And not only with regard to an entire speech, but also with individual words; these, too, seem to me to be so ambiguous, so vague, and so easily misunderstood in comparison with genuine music, which fills the soul with a

[50] Letter of 1854.

[51] A frequent observation by Mahler, according to Bruno Walter, *Gustav Mahler* (New York: Greystone Press, 1941), 83.

[52] Quoted in Nat Shapiro, op. cit., 194.

[53] Letter to Adalbert Lindner (June 6, 1891)

[54] Quoted in Nat Shapiro, op. cit., 197.

[55] ibid., 11.

[56] Luther, Preface to Rhau's *Symphoniae iucundae* (1538).

thousand things better than words. The thoughts which are expressed to me by a piece of music which I love are not too indefinite to be put into words, but on the contrary too definite.⁵⁷

Moussorgsky:
Music is a means of communicating with people, not an aim in itself.

Edward MacDowell:
Music ... is a language, but a language of the intangible, a kind of soul-language.⁵⁸

Wagner:
Music is the speech of Passion.⁵⁹

...

It is a truth forever, that where the speech of man stops short, there Music's reign begins.⁶⁰

Hans Christian Anderson:
Where words fail, music speaks.

Leo Tolstoy:
Music is the shorthand of emotion. Emotions which let themselves be described in words with such difficulty, are directly conveyed to man in music, and in that is its power and significance.⁶¹

Listeners during the nineteenth century had become fully conditioned to hear music as a synonymous expression of feeling. From an endless supply of possible quotations, consider only these two remarkable testimonies to the experience of hearing the music of Mozart.

Tchaikovsky:
Here are things which can bring tears to our eyes. I will only mention the adagio of the D minor string quintet. No one else has ever known as well how to interpret so exquisitely in music the sense of resigned and inconsolable sorrow. Every time Laub played the adagio I had to hide in the farthest corner of the concert-room, so that others might not see how deeply this music affected me.⁶²

Sören Kierkegaard:
I am in love with Mozart like a young girl. Immortal Mozart! I owe you everything; it is thanks to you that I lost my reason, that my soul was awestruck in the very depths of my being ... I have you to thank that I did not die without having loved.⁶³

⁵⁷ Letter to Marc André Souchay (October 5, 1842).

⁵⁸ *Critical and Historical Essays* (1912).

⁵⁹ Wagner, 'Judaism in Music.'

⁶⁰ Wagner, 'A Happy Evening.'

⁶¹ Quoted in Nat Shapiro, op. cit., 199.

⁶² Letter to von Meck, March 16, 1878.

⁶³ *Either/Or* (1843).

Herbert von Karajan, 'master of the recorded cult which has purged the spirit from the music'.

Nevertheless, three thousand years of experience were not enough to discourage radical new departures during the twentieth century. One new school of composers championed 'objective' music, which had never ever existed before. Their credo was that music can be understood only as C#s and Bbs. For the most part, however, the composers of 'objective' music found their greatest admirers and followers among the academic community and not among the general public, who never responded as it did for traditional music. For the general public there is not a single work from this school which communicates as directly as the weakest Beethoven symphony.

The twelve-tone school was, of course, a return to math, in so far as the process was concerned. This school is now completely dead and nearly forgotten. It lasted exactly as long as the Classic Period, which produced numerous masterpieces which will be performed forever. How many compositions from the fifty years of twelve-tone music will be performed forever? Try to count them!

Another significant new influence of the twentieth century has been the recording industry, which has made technical accuracy a higher goal than feeling. The impact of this influence can be clearly seen in the criticism of the later recordings by Karajan. Peter Davis, in *New York Magazine*, called Karajan,

> master of the recorded cult which has purged the spirit from the music.

A senior British critic considered the absence of feeling in a Karajan performance of the Beethoven *Eroica* as amounting to fraud.

> Beauty without form, sound without meaning, power without reason, reason without soul—it is the deadly logic of hi-fi. Machines, we are told, will one day compose symphonies. At present they merely perform them.

And still today we hear some concerts and recordings which are characterized by great demonstrations of technical skill and precision but lacking in genuine feeling.

And that is because we are hearing *exactly* what we teach!

4 *Music Education Must Be Experiential*

CONSIDER A FEW BENCHMARKS on the progress of American Music Education since the 1950s:

Item: During the 1970s the participation of high school students in music courses declined from 25.1 to 21.6 percent, and fell even more during the 1980s.[1]

[1] *The American School Board Journal*, December, 1988, 15.

Item: A 1985 survey by the National Endowment for the Arts found:
- 61% of adults do not attend one cultural event per year
- 68% say their parents never listened to classical music
- 80% say they never had music appreciation courses.

But!
- 57 million (1 out of 4) were playing an instrument
- Sales of music recordings were at an all time high.

Item: The Report of the National Commission on Music Education (Reston: MENC, 1991) provided some very disturbing information about our country's progress in art education.

- Of the 29 states requiring some instruction in music and the other arts for graduation, 13 accept courses in domestic science, industrial arts, humanities, foreign languages, or computer science as alternative ways to meet the requirement. Only 9 states require arts courses per se for all high school students.

- The six broad education goals advanced by President Bush and the nation's governors in 1990 do not mention the arts.

- The US government is willing to spend on support for the arts only .095% of what it spends on support for science.

- In student–teacher ratio in music, South Dakota ranked best at 151:1; California last at 1,535:1.

- Only 15 percent of California music classes were taught by a qualified music teacher.

Item: American university music education students are given the impression by their teachers that America is a model for successful music education. An objective examination of the results of our educational system tells a different story.

- Music has never become a core subject, even though all adults will consume music their entire lives, while hardly any will use 'core subjects' like calculus.
- All children love music. Why are relative few of the entire student body found in our music classes?

From these kinds of reports, taken together with what one learns on the current state of music education in discussion with almost any public school music teacher who has been in the business twenty years or more, one can only conclude that American Music Education has failed dramatically during the past fifty years. How is this to be explained?

Beginning with the late Renaissance the influence of humanism caused the professional art music field to return to the values of the ancient Greeks in which music was understood to be performance, and its paramount purpose to be the communication of feeling. At the very same time, however, the universities of Europe continued on the wrong track they had inherited from their Catholic Church sponsors, making music a branch of mathematics in order to qualify it as a rational and conceptual subject like other university subjects.

The universities generally remained locked in the old medieval Scholastic notion that music belonged to mathematics. Thus, in 1505, the University of Leipzig appointed Sebastianus Müchelon as '*lector musicae et aritmetice*,'[2] a document of the University of Köln in 1515 specifies the teaching of 'the books on mathematics, that is geometry, arithmetic, music and astronomy' and in 1558 the University of Heidelberg employed a lecturer in mathematics who was expected to include music in his teaching.

The most influential of the radical English religious books which attack music is Stephen Gosson's *The Schoole of Abuse* of 1579, which declares that the student must forget performance and return to the study of 'speculative music,' meaning what we call music theory today. First, he quotes Pythagoras, in

[2] Nan Cooke Carpenter, *Music in the Medieval and Renaissance Universities* (Norman: University of Oklahoma Press, 1958), 251. Carpenter documents the association with mathematics extensively.

something the philosopher surely never said, as 'condemning as fools, anyone who judges Music by sound and by ear.' Then, he concludes,

> If you wish to be good Scholars, and to profit from the Art of Music, shut your fiddle cases.³

A French philosopher, Nicholas Malebranche (1638–1715), writes that music can only be judged by conceptual knowledge, not by the ear. Hence he concludes, 'Musicians know nothing.'⁴

We are happy to report that some humanists satirized these old-fashioned and incorrect views. Ben Jonson, in his *Cynthia's Revels* (act 2, scene 3) in a humorous discussion of the facial expressions needed by a courtier, satirizes the pedagogy of the academic world by referring to a courier who only knows 'the court by speculation rather than through practice.' This uninformed courtier, we are told, doesn't know the '*ut-re-me-fa-sol-la* of courtship.'

In 'The Blind as Judges of Color,' Voltaire presents a brief story of the blind in a hospital who pretend to be authorities on color. This is a satire on self-proclaimed academic experts, who know nothing of a practical nature. In particular he was thinking of the Scholastic views of the University of Paris, which held that one can only 'know' music in its conceptual form ('speculative music') rather than by the ear. This story concludes with the observation by a deaf man that the 'deaf were the only proper judges of music.'⁵ Petrarch, in his 'Remedies for Fortune Fair and Foul' (II, xcvii), comments in satire of the old Church position:

> A deaf person can know the tones and numbers characterizing the intervals of fifth and octave, as well as the other proportions of the musical scale with which musicians work. Although one does not hear the sounds of the human voice, of strings or the organ, he nevertheless may understand in his mind their fundamental canon and, doubtless, will prefer the intellectual pleasure to a mere titillation of the ear.

³ Stephen Gosson, *The Schoole of Abuse* (1579), ed., Edward Arber (London, 1868), 26

⁴ Nicolas Malebranche, *Elucidations of the Search after Truth*, quoted in Malebranche, *Philosophical Selections*, trans., Thomas Lennon and Paul Olscamp (Indianapolis: Hacket Publishing Company, 1992), 89.

English playwright, poet, and actor Ben Jonson (1572–1637) by George Vertue after Gerard van Honthorst, 1730

⁵ 'The Blind as Judges of Color,' in *The Works of Voltaire* (New York: St. Hubert Guild, 1901), IV, 13ff.

One is amazed at the number of otherwise brilliant minds who continued to think of music as a branch of mathematics. The list includes Shakespeare,[6] Mersenne,[7] Isaac Newton,[8] Defoe[9] and Samuel Pepys.[10] Even in the nineteenth century one finds Hegel writing of music that,

> besides the deepest feeling, there reigns also a rigorous mathematical intelligence.[11]

Music education in young, protestant America began without obligation to the long heritage of European universities and consequently enjoyed a good start. The early church schools were practical, and not academic, in purpose. When the broader forms of public music education began to grow during the nineteenth century, America had the lucky chronological coincidence to be under strong European influence at a time when European music and music education values were completely experiential in nature. It is one reason why important nineteenth-century American music educators, such as Lowell Mason, understood and stressed the moral values of music.

During the first decades of the twentieth century, which saw the great expansion of public school music, the driving force were leaders who were performers and conductors. Some of the greatest leaders were even without formal education in music, but were dedicated to performance. The music conferences were organized around concerts by the finest models and the model was performance. This was a period of great growth in music education and strong civic support.

After World War II the entire philosophy of music education in America began to change. Music education began to be dominated not by performers of music, but by professional educators, persons with an EdD. These professional educators returned to the late medieval university model, centering the discussion on concepts and math (now called statistics) rather than performance. They began to make music like the other conceptual core subjects, rather than distinguishing its originality.

But there are fundamental problems with concept based music teaching, the first of which is that the student is led to understand music from the perspective of the teacher, rather

[6] *The Taming of the Shrew*, II, ii, 57.

[7] *Harmonie universelle* (1636).

[8] In his ideal university curriculum music is taught by the mathematics lecturer. See *Unpublished Scientific Papers of Isaac Newton*, ed., Rupert Hall (Cambridge: University Press, 1962), 369ff.

[9] Daniel Defoe, 'Augusta Triumphans: or, the Way to make London the Most Flourishing City in the Universe.'

[10] *Private Correspondence of Samuel Pepys*, ed., J. Tanner (London: Bell and Sons, 1926), II, 109.

[11] Quoted in Nat Shapiro, *An Encyclopedia of Quotations about Music* (New York: Da Capo, 1977), 276.

than from his own perspective—where *his* understanding of music must, in the end, lie. This is exactly the point Schumann makes in a note in his Diary in thinking about theory teachers. They are, he says,

> not satisfied when a young student works out the old classic form, as a master, and according to his own understanding of it; he must do so according to theirs.[12]

Robert Schumann, Wien, 1839

The result will always be that the gifted student finds frustration, not enlightenment, in being forced to write music by someone else's rules. Schumann himself was particularly sensitive to criticism of parallel fifths.

> For all I care, the fifths may ascend or descend chromatically, the melody may be doubled in every interval in octaves, but …! Yes, recently I heard in a dream angelic music filled with heavenly fifths, and this happened because, the angels assured me, they had never found it necessary to study thorough bass.[13]

Berlioz, in an article on the music of Gluck, tells of a similar anecdote about Beethoven.

> Though Gluck was not, strictly speaking, the equal of some of those who came after him, he was certainly enough of a musician to have the right of answering his critics as Beethoven once did:
> 'Who forbids this harmony?'
> 'Why, Fux, Albrechtsberger, and a dozen other theorists.'
> 'Well, I allow it.'[14]

Liszt also commented on this incident.

> Beethoven was quite right to assert *his right* to allow that which was forbidden by Kirnberger, Marpurg, Albrechtsberger, etc.![15]

And Liszt was quite right! It should be the student's right to write anything he *feels*. 'Rules' should come afterward, as a vehicle for the student to discover, by the comparison of his work with examples from earlier masters, the necessary musical insights. Under conceptual teaching theory we usually do this the other way around, presenting lists of rules to students who do not have the experiential background to understand

[12] Schumann's Diary, 1833 or before.

[13] Robert Schumann, 'Trios,' in *Neue Zeitschrift fur Musik* (1836).

[14] 'The *Alcestis* of Euripides' (1862).

[15] Letter to Franz Brendel, December 1, 1859.

them. The result, as Schumann says, is that later, 'The young mind must often unlearn theory, before it can be put in practice.' George Bernard Shaw was more adamant on this point:

> People would compose music skillfully enough if only there were no professors in the world.[16]

[16] *Music in London, 1890-1894.*

An even more fundamental problem is that by approaching the subject of music as a series of concepts we pretend to be teaching music, when we are not.

We say we are teaching music when we teach rhythm, but we are teaching mathematics.

We call music history a music course, but it is a history course. And the playing of records in a history class is not music—which by definition must be live. Recordings are to real music as photographs are to real people.

We say we are teaching music when we teach harmony, but we are teaching a foreign, symbolic language. And when have you heard a theory professor use words like 'pain' and 'sorrow'?

We say we are teaching music when we teach instrumental technique, but we are teaching a mechanical art.

In taking what is an experiential art and translating it into rational concepts, the result is often concepts which the student is unsuccessful in applying in actual practice. Consequently, since we teach rhythm as mathematics, the young musicians cannot *feel* rhythm. When we teach harmony as a symbolic language, the young musicians do not learn to *hear* harmony. The teaching of form is perhaps the most vivid example. We teach the sonata form, for example, as data, spreading it out on a blackboard looking like a family tree as it branches down into smaller units. And while this information is perfectly true as data, it is completely useless information. By this we mean it is information which can never be used, with the sole exception being if the student becomes a teacher of a university form class. It is useless information because neither the composer, the performer nor the listener ever experiences a sonata form as it appears on the blackboard. The sonata form is experienced as something moving through time, in the present tense,[17] from the beginning of the movement through to the end of the

[17] Stravinsky emphasizes this point, 'Music is the sole domain in which man realizes the present.' See *Chronicle of My Life* (1935).

movement. But we do not teach the perception of form sequentially. It was exactly this kind of problem which caused Mahler to remark,

> It is a peculiarity of the interpretation of works of art that the rational element in them is almost never their true reality.[18]

Thus in turning music into rational concepts we take the precious voice of our experiential self and turn it from *feeling* into *concepts*; from *us* into *it*; from the wordless into words; and from the right hemisphere to the left hemisphere. In fact, we are teaching everything except *music*. Here is an illustration:

> When we talk about concept learning, however, we move into the cognitive domain, where our interest is in helping students develop their thinking processes …
>
> People perform essentially three different kinds of thinking or knowing operations. The first of these, and undoubtedly the most critical, is discrimination, which is the ability to tell that one thing isn't another …
>
> The second thought operation is sequence learning—placing things in a particular order so that one event or object or situation naturally follows the preceding one …
>
> Concept formation—the third type of thought operation—is the ability to identify those characteristics that classify otherwise dissimilar objects or events.[19]

Aesthetics, which belong to the realm of the listener–student, in conceptual theory now becomes an aspect of teaching. In our view, nothing could be more wrong-headed than the following:

> [The] teacher–director will find his aesthetic attitude constantly challenged in the selection of didactic materials, in problems of musical description, and in related matters of value both as voiced by the experiencing subject and as embodied within the musical object. He is in a singular position to introduce into contexts of performance practical applications of aesthetic theories: of play, empathy, imagery, psychical distance. The actual shaping of sounds, the dramatic unfolding of musical form, the consideration of immediate and refined judgments, values, and responses—all could take on pedagogical import via the performance–analysis process.[20]

Gustav Mahler (1860–1911)

[18] Alma Mahler, *Gustav Mahler* (New York: Viking Press, 1969), 320.

[19] James C. Carlsen, 'Concept Learning—It Starts with a Concept of Music,' *Music Educators Journal*, November, 1973.

[20] Abraham A. Schwadron, 'Music Education and Teacher Preparation,' *Journal of Musicological Research*, 1982.

Such philosophizing in music education is in reality the philosophy of education or of learning, but not the philosophy of *music* education. Such conceptual efforts have often resulted in a considerable waste of human effort. Consider the fact that American music education went through a brief period of flirting with the ideas of the dehumanizing behaviorists—ten years after the field of psychology itself had finished considering and had dismissed the whole idea. This was followed with much fanfare by the era of 'Comprehensive Musicianship.' Never has a movement in music education been so short lived, leaving closets all over the country filled with unused publications paid for by government grants.

The result of nearly a half-century of conceptual music teaching is declining numbers of music students, relative to the population, with little discernible civic support. The reason for this, a reason intuitively grasped by students and parents alike, is that music is not a conceptual subject, it is experiential. A conceptual philosophy of music education can only mean teaching *about* music, not teaching *music*.

This is the first problem when we conceptualize music. These things are the rational, left hemisphere associations with music. They are necessary to write the notes on paper and we use them as means of conceptualizing about music. But they are not *music*. This is the point once made by the German poet, Heine:

> Nothing is more futile than theorizing about music. No doubt there are laws, mathematically strict laws, but these laws are not music; they are only its conditions—just as the art of drawing and the theory of colors, even the brush and palette, are not painting, but only its necessary means. The essence of music is revelation; it does not admit of exact reckoning.[21]

Mahler adds the warning that conceptualizing, placing the focus on what you can talk about, only serves to mislead us and distract one from what is important in music.

> It is a peculiarity of the interpretation of works of art that the rational element in them is almost never their true reality.[22]

[21] Heinrich Heine, 'Letters on the French Stage' (1837).

[22] Alma Mahler, *Gustav Mahler* (New York: Viking Press, 1969), 320.

Saint-Saëns reminds us of the very obvious fact that the reverse is also true: music cannot communicate rational ideas. The question follows, if music cannot convey concepts, why do we think we can explain music by concepts?

> Nothing is more difficult than to speak about music. The attempt is very arduous for musicians themselves and nearly impossible for others ...
>
> I have invariably found this art by nature unable to convey purely abstract ideas ... whereas, on the contrary, music is all-powerful when it comes to expressing the several degrees of passion, the infinite nuances of feeling. Insight into the soul, the exploration of its inmost recesses, is precisely its most congenial task, the scene of its triumphant success. Music takes up where speech leaves off, it utters the ineffable, makes us discover in ourselves depths we had not suspected, conveys impressions and states of being that no words can render.[23]

[23] *Portraits et Souvenirs* (1903).

The teaching of *music* can *only* occur through the performance of music, including in the classroom and in rehearsals, because music does not exist except in performance. But this is a form of music education for which university teacher training does not prepare its students. Consider the average school band rehearsal. The band plays for a few moments, then stops while the conductor makes comments. Then they play for a while and stop again, play and stop, etc. Ironically, all of current music educational theory is focused on *the intervals where there is no music.*

We should like to propose that the focus of music education needs to be returned to direct experience in the *playing* of music. Conceptual teaching is important only in its supporting role, but it must never be confused with the core values of music teaching. Otherwise, Wagner concluded,

> If one needs a science for it, then Art is useless.[24]

[24] William Ashton Ellis, *Wagner's Prose Works* (New York: Broude, VIII, 392.

Real music education must be learned through personal experience, not through the contemplation of concepts and math. History is very rich in teachers of this basic truth. Leonardo da Vinci (1452–1519), for example, observed,

> To me it seems that all sciences are vain and full or errors that are not born of experience, mother of all certainty, and that are not tested by experience.[25]

[25] Jean Paul Richter, ed., *The Literary Works of Leonardo da Vinci* (London: Phaidon, 1970), I, 33ff.

The greatest French writer of the sixteenth century, Michel Montaigne (1533–1592), ridicules those who think they can teach experiential arts, such as music and dance, through conceptual teaching alone.[26] Extending this thought in humor, he quotes Plato[27] as saying we should never submit ourselves to a doctor unless he himself had had the same illness and cured himself. Thus, says Montaigne,

> If doctors want to know how to cure syphilis it is right that they should first catch it themselves!

Erasmus (1469–1536) calls practice, 'the best teacher of any subject,' with the specific example, that one learns music by playing.[28] In this regard, Franchino Gaffurio (1451–1518), in his *Practica musicae*, notes that performing musicians had been ignoring the academic *musica speculativa* anyway. But having come from this latter tradition himself, he is somewhat astonished that musicians could learn such things as harmony without the conceptual instruction.

> It is incredible that musicians could have attained the practical skill in harmony which they did attain without any study of theory.[29]

Gaffurio's explanation for this 'incredible' fact is the correct one: musicians learn the fundamentals of music experientially.[30]

The Flemish theorist Adrian Coclico, a music teacher at the university in Wittenberg in 1545, documents in his *Compendium Musices* (1552) actual examples of the sixteenth-century shift away from the old Scholastic complexities of speculative music to practical musicianship.[31] He mentions that in Belgian cities no music is written down or prescribed by precept. Especially interesting is his reference to his own training:

> My teacher, Josquin des Près, never rehearsed or wrote out any musical procedures, yet in a short time made perfect musicians, since he did not hold his students back in long and frivolous precepts, but taught precepts in a few words at the same time as singing through exercise and practice.[32]

---

[26] Michel de Montaigne, *Essays*, trans., M. A. Screech (London: Penguin, 1993), I, xxvi, 171.

[27] *Republic*, III, 408 D-E.

[28] 'Adages,' in *The Collected Works of Erasmus* (Toronto: University of Toronto Press, 1992), XXXII, 25.

[29] Irwin Young, trans., *The Practica musicae of Franchinus Gafurius* (Madison: University of Wisconsin Press, 1969),11.

[30] It is this same explanation, we might add, that accounts for the fact that the world is filled with musicians who have never taken music classes!

[31] In Adrian Coclico, *Musical Compendium*, trans., Albert Seay (Colorado Springs: Colorado College Music Press, 1973), 30.

[32] ibid., 16.

The Baroque writers were even more outspoken against the old academic *musica speculativa*. Johann Mattheson (1681–1764) begins his first important book, *Das Neu-Eröffnete Orchestre*, with a startling chapter entitled, 'the Fall of Music and its Cause.' His basic view was that music is something very close to Nature, but the student is led to believe that he knows nothing of music unless he knows the academic conceptual form of it. Mattheson writes of these professors:

'Critica Musica' by Johann Mattheson

> For they are persuaded that this beautiful and perfect creation, which a beneficent God has given us men for our pleasure, and likewise as a model of the eternal, harmonious Splendor, depends solely upon deep learning and laborious knowledge. To prove this, they dispense their philosophical rules and scholarly vagaries, not only with great authority, but likewise with such obscurity that one has a rightful aversion for the stuff, and would rather remain in permanent ignorance than to go through such *horrenda*.[33]

33 *Das Neu-Eröffnete Orchestre*, in Beekman Cannon, *Johann Mattheson, Spectator in Music* (Archon Books, 1968), 2ff.

In another place he argues that those concepts which are necessary should be centered in performance.

> That type of contemplation or theory is however to be preferred to all others which does not delve so deeply into shallow, mental considerations that action is forgotten; but turns its main aim toward actual practice and usage … Whoever wants to make good use of both aspects must never separate them, but keep them fast together, like body and soul.[34]

34 Johann Mattheson, *Der vollkommene Capellmeister* (1739), trans., Ernest Harris (Ann Arbor: UMI Research Press, 1981), I, i, 5.

He observes that while it is an intelligent thing to ponder, contemplate and reflect on a piece of music before performing it, it sometimes works the other way around. That is, the study seems to be a 'corroboration of that which one finds to be true in practice.' The same conclusion is given by King James I, in his book of advice to his son 'that Art is better learned by practice than speculation.'[35]

35 James I, *Basilicon Doron* (1599) (Menston: Scolar Press, 1969), 67.

Two Baroque writers emphasize that musical understanding does not come from books. Fénelon (1651–1715), thinking of the listener, observes that one does not learn music from books, but from observing musicians.[36] And in a letter to Père Porée, Voltaire (1694–1778) also contends that the artist learns by experience, and not from books.

36 François de Salignac de La Mothe-Fénelon, *The Adventures of Telemachus, Son of Ulysses*, Book XII, (London: Garland Publishing, 1979, facsimile of the 1720 edition), XXIV, ii, 270.

> No matter how many books are written on the technique of painting by those who know their subject, not one of them will afford as much instruction to the pupil as will the sight of a single head by Raphael.
>
> The principles of all the arts, which depend upon imagination, are simple and easy; they are based upon nature and reason ... The composer of *Armide* and *Issé* [Lully], and the worst of composers, worked according to the same musical rules.[37]

By the end of the Baroque, we see Charles Avison (1709–1770), in a complete break with Scholastic dogma, state that musical communication is *not* of the realm of Reason.

> After all that has been, or can be said, the energy and grace of musical expression is of too delicate a nature to be fixed by words: it is a matter of taste, rather than of reasoning, and is, therefore, much better understood by example than by precept.[38]

The great value of music is that its revelation is on a *personal* level. Joseph Campbell wrote about how the importance of personal revelation is lost in academic conceptualization.

> People talk about trying to learn the meaning of life. Life has no meaning. What's the meaning of a flower? What we are looking for is an experience of life, getting the experience. But we're shoving ourselves off the experience by naming, translating and classifying every experience that comes to us.[39]

And this is what Debussy had in mind, when he wrote, 'Music must never be shut in and become an academic art.'[40] Aaron Copland presented a great lesson on this importance of personal revelation in music.

> Listen ... to the forty-eight fugue themes of Bach's Well-Tempered Clavichord. Listen to each theme, one after another. You will soon realize that each theme mirrors a different world of feeling. You will also soon realize that the more beautiful a theme seems to you the harder it is to find any word that will describe it to your complete satisfaction. Yes, you will certainly know whether it is a gay theme or a sad one ... Now study the sad one a little closer. Try to pin down the exact quality of its sadness. Is it pessimistically or resignedly sad; is it fatefully sad or smilingly sad? Let us suppose that you are fortunate and can describe to your own satisfaction in so many words the exact meaning of your chosen theme. There is still no guarantee that anyone else will be satisfied. Nor need they be. The important thing is that each one feel for himself

[37] Letter to Père Porée (1730), quoted in Barrett Clark, *European Theories of the Drama* (New York: Crown, 1959), 279.

English eighteenth-century composer Charles Avison

[38] Charles Avison, *An Essay on Musical Expression* [London, 1753] (New York: Broude Reprint, 1967), 81.

[39] Joseph Campbell, *Transformations of Myth Through Time* (New York: Harper & Row, 1990), 204ff. With regard to how the academic world often fails to connect its precepts with real life, Robert Ornstein, responding to a friend's question about taping a box, suggested using 'the Pythagorean theorem and compute the length of the diagonal compared with the sum of the two sides.' His friend responded, 'Is that what geometry was all about? [Robert Ornstein, *The Right Mind* (New York: Harcourt Brace, 1997), 171]

[40] Quoted in Nat Shapiro, *An Encyclopedia of Quotations About Music* (New York, Da Capo, 1977), 268.

the specific expressive quality of a theme, or, similarly, of an entire piece of music. And if it is a great work of art, don't expect it to mean exactly the same thing to you each time you return to it.[41]

[41] Aaron Copland, *What to Listen For in Music*, Chapter 2.

Aaron Copland

We believe this is essentially what Wagner meant when he concluded, 'We cannot accept a thing conceptually if we have not already grasped it intuitively.'[42] It was for this reason that in his proposal for the design of a music school for Munich, he found that only in the context of live performance did all the conceptual teaching make sense.

[42] Letter to August Röckel (August 23, 1856).

> The invisible bond, uniting the various branches of study, will always have to be performance.[43]

[43] 'A Music School for Munich,' William Ellis, *Wagner's Prose Works* (New York: Broude), IV, 197.

In summary, in the United States of America we do not teach *music* education.
We teach the grammar of music.
We teach the activities which use music.

But we do not teach *music*. Music is a language for the communication of feeling. That is all music is, that is all music has ever been. This fact has been documented for three thousand years by scholars of all kinds and is evident on the basis of common sense. Anything else that can be discussed on the topic of music may have relative levels of importance, but it is not music.

We teach the technique of the performance of music—how to play correct pitches in the right time and at the right dynamic level.

We teach the grammar of music, with questionable success.

We do not teach the communication of feeling and emotion. We do not discuss the feelings and emotions with the student. The student is left to discover and experience his emotional template outside the school building.

The general student body, reflecting society itself, is interested in music *only* in its association with emotion, in performance either as a listener or as a potential player or composer.

Therefore, at present, relatively few students are in our music classes.

They are utterly bored with the 'concepts' of music.

They want involvement in music; they are not interested in merely learning *about* music.

    Because we do not teach what music really is and because we do not teach what young people want and are attracted to in music, the following must be confessed by any objective observer.

    Other than being in the band or choir, and that may largely be for social reasons, public school students are not filling our classes, even though music is something they *all* love. That is an extraordinary fact to consider. In a society where many, perhaps a majority, of students do not like school (and vast numbers drop out) they do *not* elect classes in the one subject they love!

    These students become adults who place little or no importance in having good music be part of their lives. They rarely go to concerts, other than pop concerts. In other words, what we have done in school has contributed no high moral or ethical values to their lives. Hence they become citizens exposed to the lowest values associated with popular music. Are you satisfied with the contribution such music has made in our society and how it has shaped our society?

Since these adults have had to find music for themselves and place no value on the conceptual experience they received in school, they will not support 'music education' beyond following their children to observe their activities.

Surely one can see the futility and waste of time, effort and money in today's concept-based music education for their monuments stand in every city, large or small. We must abandon the failed concept-based experiments of the second half of the twentieth century and return music education to the fundamental experiential values which were so successful across so many earlier centuries.

Music is for the ear, not the eye.

There is much to suggest there is an innate musicality in virtually everyone.

...

It is not always easy or possible for children to receive musical training, especially in the United States, where music instruction is being eliminated from many public schools.[1]

Dr. Oliver Sacks, 2007

5   *Music Education Must Educate All Children*

FOR MANY YEARS PHILOLOGISTS HAVE REASONED that music came before speech. Today there is a great deal of interest in clinical medicine that contemplates the role of perfect pitch, or 'absolute pitch,' in very early man. If, in a time before language, a group of people depended on a kind of musical humming to express a range of emotions the existence of perfect pitch may have been a necessary component of communication. That is, perfect pitch among all group members might be necessary to distinguish the difference between mere fear and 'the tiger is at the door of the cave.'

Among the most striking findings relative to early man's contribution to us today are those which have to do with the acquisition of absolute pitch or 'perfect pitch.'

> There is evidence that almost all musicians who began their training before the age of 6 possess absolute pitch, compared with none of those who began after the age of 11.[2]

Dr. Sacks quotes a similar study by Hamilton, Pascual-Leone and Schlaug who found that musical training before the age of six or eight was a key to preserving absolute pitch,[3] which otherwise seems to get pushed into the background when the language function of the left-hemisphere begins to become dominant.

On the other hand the nature of the demands of language in some cultures seems to preserve absolute pitch to some degree. A study by Diana Deutsch, a scholar who has made tremendous progress in the study of hearing music, points to the critical demands of pitch among speakers of Vietnamese and Mandarin. She made a study of first-year students at the Eastman School of Music and of the Central Conservatory of Music in Beijing which resulted in very interesting findings. For students who began music instruction between ages four and five approximately 60% of the Chinese students met the criterion for absolute pitch compared to only 14% of the US. For those beginning the study of music at age six or seven the

[1] Dr. Oliver Sacks, *Musicophilia* (New York: Knopf, 2007), 95, and 95, fn. 4.

[2] D. Sergeant, 'Experimental Investigation of Absolute Pitch,' in *Journal of Research in Musical Education*, 1969, 17, 135-143.

[3] Sacks, op. cit., 163.

corresponding figures were 55% and 6%. For those who began music study at age eight or nine the corresponding figures were 42% and 0%.

The conclusion seems to be that it is the residual genetic absolute pitch which is needed to form language ability and then is lost according to the pitch requirements of the language in question. Deutsch thinks that perhaps 'enabling infants to associate pitches with verbal labels during the critical period might help all infants acquire absolute pitch.'[4]

It is fair to say that clinical medicine has now concluded, through natural laws, such as the overtone series, through the 'musical' experiences passed down from earliest man and through the evolution of the close association of music and emotions in the right hemisphere of our brains, we are a species genetically pre-wired to understand music as a language. All mankind, including infants, understand music and they understand this language without instruction. It is therefore no surprise that the man on the street will swear to you he 'can't carry a tune,' but will then get into his truck and listen to music all the way home.

Dr. Sacks points to the well-known Suzuki method to teach young children entirely by ear and by imitation to play the violin. He notes that 'virtually all hearing children respond to such training'[5] as another indication of the genetic musical information which comes with us all at birth. I might add that many years ago I had a conversation in Japan with a leading man in the Suzuki program and he told me their goal was to produce a society in which every person could play a Mozart violin or a Mozart piano concerto. 'Our goal,' he said, 'is not to produce musicians, but to build better Japanese.'

This amazing genetic background is ignored once man enters school. We have constructed a school system designed to educate half a brain, literally. In school we ignore music even though it is universal in nature and will be fundamental to, and in daily use by, all people for the duration of their lives and we make a 'core subject' of calculus which hardly anyone will ever use after leaving school.

For a long time in the United States of America we have gone further and transformed what we call *music* education into something which is not music at all. We have focused our music education on knowing *about* music, rather than knowing

[4] ibid., 127.

[5] ibid.

music. Unfortunately, we have therefore succeeded in creating a general public that believes that if you don't know anything *about* music, then you don't know anything about *music*. In addition to this we have created the notion that some children are 'talented,' by which we mean nothing whatsoever about understanding music, only the identification of children with relatively advanced performance skills. The member of the public who does not play an instrument is therefore encouraged to understand that he has no aptitude for music.

In this way, we have created people who believe music is not for everyone. For example, the holder of a Nobel Prize in Physics, Paul Dirac, said,

> Just like beauty in a picture or beauty in music. You can't describe it, it's something—and if you don't feel it, you just have to accept that you're not susceptible to it. No one can explain it to you. If someone doesn't appreciate the beauty of music, what can you do? Give 'em up!"[6]

[6] Quoted by Horace F. Judson, 'Where Einstein and Picasso Meet,' *Newsweek*, November 17, 1980.

An even more extraordinary, and misinformed, view is Langer's:

> Great art is not a direct sensuous pleasure. If it were, it would appeal—like cake or cocktails—to the untutored as well as to the cultured taste.[7]

[7] S. K. Langer, *Philosophy in a New Key* (Cambridge: Harvard University, 3rd ed.,1976), 205.

This is all completely wrong, of course! Every one of our species is born with a genetic affinity to understand music. Period! Music has been a part of man longer than anything else—longer than speech, or houses or clothes. But beyond that, studies demonstrate that in the fetus the right hemisphere develops earlier than the left and response to sound appears as early as twenty-four weeks after conception.[8]

The actual affinity for a musical language can also be tested at a very early age. Dennis Molfese of the University of Pennsylvania has conducted studies on infants less than forty-eight hours after birth.

[8] Clinical research sources given in Michael C. Corballis, *The Lopsided Ape* (New York: Oxford University Press, 1991), 296, 299. The left hemisphere experiences a growth spurt between ages two and four.

> University of Pennsylvania psychologist Dennis Molfese conducted studies on infants less than 48 hours after birth, to investigate their hemispheric organization. Using EEG monitoring, he measured each infant's hemispheric response to a continuous loop of five variously ordered sounds—two synthetically produced speech syllables, two non-speech sounds constructed of pure tones within the central frequency range of human speech and one pure tone just flat of middle C.

Molfese discovered that the left hemisphere responded more strongly to speech syllables, while the right hemisphere showed a stronger response to nonspeech sounds.[9]

[9] Craig Buck, 'Knowing the LEFT from the RIGHT,' *Human Behavior*, June, 1976.

University of California researchers believe that infants are born with a genetic ability to recognize and respond to music, even before language.

It is known that infants recognize and respond to music, and the UC Irvine scientists believe that is because humans are born with certain brain cells that respond to musical sounds.

These neurons work in patterns that can be expanded as a sort of 'pre-language' to perform increasingly complex interactions—even before the brain has developed verbal language skills, physicist Gordon Shaw said.

This ability may bolster higher level thinking skills … we think this ability is going to be a very useful tool in any kind of higher brain activity.[10]

[10] *Associated Press*, January 23, 1992.

Psychologists have found that even before age *one*, infants can detect errors in music!

Studies of the musical abilities of children suggest that this wiring up of the brain's musical knowledge begins very early in life and, like language, is specific to a particular culture. Experiments by psychologist Sandra Trehub of the University of Toronto suggest that even infants possess a rudimentary ability to distinguish whether particular chords contain a wrong note. Psychologist Michael Lynch of the University of Miami found that by age one children were better at recognizing changes in a particular melody when the notes were drawn from a scale in conventional Western music as opposed to melodies written from a scale common in Indonesia.[11]

[11] 'The Musical Brain,' *U. S. News & World Report*, June 11, 1990.

Dr. Lynch is wrong, however, in his conclusion that this is culture driven; it is nature driven, from the natural overtone structure of all sound.

These scientists warn us that for the musical language, as with any other kind of language, it is the early years, perhaps before age seven, which is the most fruitful for education.

There may be critical periods for the development of different talents, some experts believe. Music and foreign languages can be learned very readily at an early age, but later these subjects become more difficult. If there are critical periods for the development of the right hemisphere's mechanical ingenuity, for instance, it may be necessary to train it at that age or lose forever the possibility of realizing its full potential.[12]

[12] Wayne Sage, 'The Split Brain Lab,' *Human Behavior*, June, 1976.

Regarding emotions, so inseparable from music, it has long been observed that infants immediately recognize the emotional language of the face (and voice) and without any instruction.

Early in life infants can distinguish facial expression, and they can remember facial expressions following brief exposure. As the infant matures, she becomes sensitive to faces, words, and gestures by caregivers. Babies become attuned to the people who will help them. There is an almost amazing mesh between the individual's development and his or her world. Children can recognize emotions without having seen them before.[13]

[13] Robert Ornstein, *The Evolution of Consciousness* (New York: Prentice Hall, 1991), 100.

Furthermore, infants who are born blind and deaf make the same facial expressions as normal infants, which indicates once again that emotional patterns are genetic and not learned.

Consider children who are born both deaf and blind. One would think that they had little chance to pattern their behavior through observation of others ... Blind and deaf children, none the less, smile, laugh, weep, stamp their feet, clench their fists and frown like normal children. A second group of interest are the mentally retarded. 'Even severely mentally handicapped children smile, laugh and weep although it is impossible, even with great effort to teach them to eat with a spoon. It is unthinkable that they could have learned these complicated motor patterns, when failing in tasks that are much simpler.'[14]

[14] Neil McNaughton, *Biology and Emotion* (Cambridge University Press, 1989), 43; I. Eibl-Eibesfeldt, *Love and Hate* (London: Methuen, 1971; and Charles Darwin, *The Expression of Emotions in Man and Animals* (London: Friedmann, 1979), 352.

Ornstein's discussion of the early development of emotions points again to this vital early period. It seems obvious to me that it is *this* period when music *should* be introduced into the life of all children.

Since we are equipped for action, not comprehensive understanding, our brain seeks significance, not specific bits of information. We learn general semblances of the world, just enough to get by. That's why we don't, can't, store the zillion ways we could write or communicate *I took the cat out* not to mention the billion other sentences we could think of immediately.

During early development nerve cells compete with one another to survive, to connect into working groups, so that they persevere. If cells are given a certain kind of stimulation, some connect to others and form neural groups; if not, they conjoin with others. Because of experiences early on in the world, the nervous system gets wired up in different ways.

[15] ibid., 126.

Consequently, individuals have different brains because of their early experiences. Of course, later development can also have an effect. Early experiences, especially those of deprivation, can be overcome, and later experiences, such as the shock of battle, can dramatically and permanently change the nature of the brain. But it is in the first years that most of the world's selection of the mind takes place.[15]

It seems beyond question that all infants and young children have an affinity for music. Children become adults and even those adults who might call themselves non-musicians also carry genetic information on music. Indeed, a recent review in the *New York Times* cites a researcher, Daniel Levitin, who concludes,

> By the age of 5 we are all musical experts, so this stuff is clearly wired really deeply into us.[16]

[16] Clive Thompson, *Music of the Hemispheres* (2006), reviewed in the *New York Times*, Oct. 29, 2007.

In a little casual test of how much musical ability remained with ordinary adults, Dr. Levitin stopped people on the street and asked them to sing, entirely from memory, one of their favorite hit songs. The results were astonishingly accurate. Most people could hit the tempo of the original song within a 4% margin of error and two-thirds of the people sang within a semitone of the original pitch of the song.

Some recent research at Ohio State clearly also demonstrates the inherent abilities of the 'non-musician.'

> Recent experiments that tested non-musicians' musical skills dramatically illustrate that most people have an exquisitely crafted musical sense that has developed subconsciously over their lifetimes, even if they can't know Mozart from Madonna. Music theorist David Butler of Ohio State University's School of Music found that listeners with no musical training can nevertheless indicate by whistling or choosing from a set of tones which of the 12 possible pitch keys a piece of music is in, sometimes after hearing only a few sample notes. Butler suggests that people subconsciously know through experience that particular combinations of notes occur only in certain keys and gradually narrow the possibilities as more combinations of notes are heard.
>
> This 'hidden' knowledge in the mind may arise as a natural consequence of how the brain's neurons change the communication pathways among themselves in response to experience, says Dartmouth's Bharu-

cha. Working with a computer model of brain cells called a neural network, Bharucha found that as he exposed the model to music, the layer of brain cells responsible for processing individual notes sent signals to another layer whose cells gradually became specialized for recognizing specific groups of notes, or chords. These cells in turn signaled a third layer of cells that gradually became responsible for recognizing groups of chords as belonging to particular keys. This hierarchical grouping occurred even though Bharucha gave the brain model no explicit instructions as to how the cells should connect themselves. Instead, the network simply organized itself in a manner that reflected the intrinsic organization of music itself.[17]

[17] 'The Musical Brain,' op. cit.

Both the ability of David Butler's subjects to ascertain the fundamental pitch note from a group of notes and what Bharucha calls 'hidden' knowledge are best explained, in my opinion, in the 'hidden' biological and genetic information we carry from being exposed to the natural overtone structure of all sounds since the earliest of time. My view of this is constantly reinforced by examples of common observation. Recently, for example, a colleague leaving for a few days asked me to take care of two large birds. One day my son, Stefan, decided to practice violin and began playing the Mendelssohn E Minor Concerto. I was quite startled to hear that by the time Stefan had played the equivalent of about half of the first page of the solo part, both birds began singing a sustained E. From hundreds of fast moving notes the birds had determined accurately the fundamental.

Even those persons who maintain they are tone deaf actually exhibit the musical elements of pitch, rhythm and cadence in their everyday speaking.

> Many people describe themselves as more or less 'tone deaf.' In fact, however, everyone can modulate his voice expressively and interpret the inflections of other voices. (Even a dog can interpret a tone of voice).[18]

[18] Manfred Clynes, 'The Pure Pulse of Musical Genius,' *Psychology Today*, July, 1974.

The nineteenth-century writer, Charles Lamb, wrote that he was tone deaf, but please don't think he doesn't appreciate music!

> When therefore I say that I have no ear, you will understand me to mean—for music. To say [however] that this heart never melted at the concord of sweet sounds, would be a foul self-libel.[19]

[19] *Essays of Elia* (1821).

I believe further that because everyone is by nature experiential, he has the ability to make perfectly aesthetic judgments regarding music (which is also experiential by nature). Even General Grant's famous comment when asked if he knew anything about music, that he could recognize two songs—one was 'Yankee Doodle' and the other wasn't—was, for him, an aesthetic observation. His statement reminds me of an occasion when I accompanied my father to a bank, where we encountered a display of very abstract paintings by a local artist. My father immediately grumbled some comment about the nature of all modern art, upon which I said, 'Yes, but among these paintings, is there one you like better than the rest?' He immediately responded, 'Well, yes, of course, I like *that one*,' as he pointed to one of the paintings.

There is no question about most people responding to music. Important questions, it seems to me, lie at the doorstep of music educators. Do we, as the professionals of music education, have an ethical responsibility to engage adults, and not just children, in a life of music? What ethics have we in determining the quality of such experiences in music? Should senior citizens, for example, be provided only with recreational music or do they have the same needs of self-discovery, creativity, etc., as children?

At present we ignore this population, we leave them to be the victims of chance, when it comes to the development of their experiences. The result is a population with the widely diverse and random sensitivities described by Wagner.

> [If there were a survey taken] we shall find that a large proportion of the audience has fallen on the theater tonight in error and from false supposition. What brought them here may certainly be gauged as nothing but the quest of entertainment, and that in the case of every comer; only, the strange diversity of receptiveness, in kind as in degree, is plainer to the physiognomical observer of a theater public than anywhere else—even than at church, since there hypocrisy conceals what here dares figure unabashed. Nor are the various grades of society and education, to which the spectators belong, by any means an index to the individual's receptiveness: in the dearest, as in the cheapest seats, one meets the same phenomenon of interest and apathy packed side by side. At one of the excellent first performances of 'Tristan' in Munich I observed a vigorous dame of middle age in the last extremity of boredom during the third act, while the cheeks of her husband, a graybeard superior officer, were streaming with tears of the deepest emotion.[20]

[20] Quoted in William Ashton Ellis, ed., *Wagner's Prose Works* (New York: Broude), VI, 63.

Are we as professional music educators content to let society be shaped by random experience? Suppose we had a society of adults who were all involved to some degree in quality musical experiences. How would that change the climate of discussion regarding the retention of music in the public schools?

If the purpose of education is to make meaning of life, then we must provide music education for all children and all adults. Music is of meaning to everyone and we must stop associating it with only the 'talented.'

Music educators are part of a very long, unbroken chain of teachers who have taken these incredible genetic gifts of music and developed them and built on them for the cultural advancement of society. How will history judge the contributions of our generation?

Music whispers to us dim secrets
that startle our wonder as to who we are.

Emerson

6 *Music Education Must Educate The Real Child*

THE MUSIC EDUCATORS NATIONAL CONFERENCE, in a 1991 publication, presented the following arguments in support of music in the public schools:

> Common sense lends support to the belief that music and music education foster a number of nonmusical factors important for success in school and life. Three areas are important here:
> 1. development goals such as self-esteem, self-discipline, and individual creativity;
> 2. the development of important academic and personal skills; and
> 3. the contributions of music to other areas of study, particularly to their integration.[1]

[1] *The Report of the National Commission on Music Education* (Reston: MENC, 1991), 23.

On the contrary, the 'common sense' of parents and administrators, all of whom carry genetic musical knowledge, tells them these things are not unique values of music at all and might as well be a list of goals for employees working in a bank. Every school board will quickly conclude that music is simply too expensive a program to maintain for the purpose of helping to instill 'self-discipline.'

These arguments for why we have music in the curriculum have a kind of desperate quality about them, like a preacher arguing for the benefits of love without being allowed to use the actual word 'love.' That is a pretty good analogy for why these kinds of arguments do not work. They are an attempt to conceptualize music, to force the left hemisphere of the brain to make up arguments even though it has no idea what goes on in the right hemisphere of the brain where the experiential nature of music lies.

We must, instead, learn to defend music in the curriculum in terms of its unique contributions to the child as an individual. This would be altogether more advantageous to us in view of the fact that most of the rest of education is designed to educate only half a brain. How could we present society a stronger defense of music in the public schools than the fact that music educates in the 'other half' of the brain which the school board has overlooked? In addition, the fact that the half-brain which is virtually ignored in education *is the half that is the real us* should make a school board very uncomfortable.

Dr. Roger Sperry, who won the Nobel Prize in Medicine for his research on the nature of bicameral human brain function, observed that American educational institutions only educate half a brain. Aside from the rather obvious suggestion implied by Dr. Sperry that the education of both hemispheres would surely be a more effective form of education, the most serious implications lie in what our species will become through educating *only* the half brain (the left hemisphere) we have chosen to educate. The half we have left out of education, the right hemisphere, is the very part of the brain which contains that part of us which is unique, unlike anyone else on earth—the *real us*. As Wagner pointed out,

> The very essence of the human species consists in the diversity of human individuality.[2]

[2] 'Eine Mittheilung an meine Freunde' (1851).

In designing educational systems which concentrate more and more on the functions of the left hemisphere, and in particular the emphasis on science in recent years, we are creating persons who, in the words of Sam Reese, 'have ceased to become whole persons.'

> Roszak has said,[3] 'There are ... other kinds of knowledge, those born of sensuous penetration, loving participation, ecstasy, transcendent aspiration. But that way lies art, joy, wisdom, salvation ...'—not science. It is time we realize that the scientific ideal of objectivity has been carried too far and has contributed to our common disease of alienation. As artists and educators, we can use the powerful ability of music to bring about nonintellectual, intuitive, experiential knowledge ...
>
> Because of the scientific ideal of objectivity, we have ceased to be whole persons. We have forgotten that we are more than an intellectual and logical apparatus, that we are also capable of feeling and sensing and participating directly in the world.[4]

[3] Theodore Roszak, *Where the Wasteland Ends* (New York: Doubleday, 1972), 196.

[4] Sam Reese, 'Discovering the Nonintellectual Self,' *Music Educators Journal*, May, 1974.

The impact of such an educational system in personal terms has been expressed in a vivid, and touching, confession by recording artist, Rosanne Cash.

> We rely heavily on logic and cognitive processes and, indeed, that is half of our condition as human beings. But the other, subtler half—the intuitive, creative part—we treat like a shameful alien cousin to our personalities ... In my own life, I spent my formative years feeling like a freak of nature, because that alien cousin was the part I completely identified with, but was not valued or validated by my teachers.[5]

[5] Quoted in *The Report of the National Commission on Music Education*, op. cit., 9.

Of that which we have left out of our school curriculum, the most significant, in terms of the development of balanced persons, is that part of us which has to do with emotions and feelings. This problem is expressed wonderfully by Burton R. Hoffman.

> Our lives are governed by our feelings. We often act on feelings of instinct or intuition. Some feelings are uneasy or unsettling. Very often someone says, 'I don't feel right about that'—a feeling he cannot quite put his finger on. Everyone daydreams and fantasizes—again, more feelings. Some emotions are recognizable and have names, but there are many feelings to which we can attach no label. Some feelings create an aura of well-being; many are puzzling and disturbing. Some feelings are difficult to control, and intelligence seems to have little deterring effect. People know they should not smoke, but they do it anyway …
>
> The arts—music, art, drama, ballet, literature, cinema, architecture—are important because they encompass every aspect of human feelings. They are perhaps the only means we have of objectifying our subjective nature …
>
> The difficulty for many people in understanding any sort of philosophy about the arts is that the arts are basically nonverbal. No matter how much we talk about them, the real import of the arts is not expressed in words; it is expressed in feelings. Although language is used, the main import of poetry is not verbal. The poet uses figures of speech to capture moments of feeling and offers us insights into our own private worlds of living, where there are no names for these experienced feelings …
>
> Although verbalization is not the main import of the arts, we do discuss them to help us get on the right track, to be receptive, to lay the groundwork for understanding. In the first grade, teachers draw on what students say they see or hear in music or what they can express with their bodies in movement when they have no words to communicate their feelings. Later, in the second, third, or fourth grades, students refine their verbalization as their attitudes and understandings change and as their skills increase. During their years in the upper grades, their ability to create, analyze, synthesize, and evaluate is highly dependent on verbalization …
>
> Unfortunately, television has almost forced us into passive roles as spectators instead of participants. This may be the fault of a misuse of the medium, not of the medium itself. Most of the images that invade our homes urge us to act without further thought. Canned laughter is even supplied so we will know when to laugh. We are urged to buy something, go somewhere, borrow money, eat, drink, or think in a certain way. We are expected to act automatically. The arts, on the other hand, actively engage us. Our whole being is involved—the mind, the senses, the human spirit …

> Children who are sent to school are entrusted to educators for the formal part of their education. Shouldn't that education include more than just acquiring skills? Learning to read is of little value in the long run if reading outside of school is confined to comic books, advertisements, and sensational literature. Most of our children's school time from now until they are graduated will be spent preparing for a job at the end. But there will be little significance to their lives if they are merely shells housing shallow personalities, devoid of humaneness in their dealings with the world.[6]

[6] Burton R. Hoffman, 'The Arts in Society and Education,' *Music Educators Journal*, March, 1973.

The need to achieve greater balance in our educational institutions is clearly urgent. Our present educational system is so completely one-sided we need not ever fear of going too far in the other direction, as pointed out by C. S. Lewis.

> For every one pupil who needs to be guarded from a weak excess of sensibility there are three who need to be awakened from the slumber of cold vulgarity. The task of the modern educator is not to cut down jungles but to irrigate deserts.[7]

[7] C. S. Lewis, *The Abolition of Man* (New York: Macmillian, 1967), 24.

I'm not sure what Lewis means here by 'a weak excess of sensibility,' but perhaps it does raise a question. For the listener of music, can there be such a thing as 'too much sensibility?' Mendelssohn debated this with a pastor in Berlin in an exchange of letters in 1833. Mendelssohn's view was,

> There is no such thing as an excess of sensibility, and what is called 'too-much' is always rather 'too-little.' The soaring, elevated emotions inspired by music—so welcome to the listeners—are no excess; let him, who is capable of emotions, feel them to the utmost of his capacity—and more so, if possible.[8]

[8] Letter to Pastor Bauer, March 4, 1833.

Whom do We Educate?—Do We Really Educate *Us*?

We have many minds, as our birthright of evolution, one of which we call *us*—our conscious self. But where is this *us*? In which of these two hemispheres, each so different and each more or less oblivious to the other, is the *us* located? The answer, of course, depends on what is meant by *us*.

Each hemisphere, in addition to the functions it performs, is a data bank. Roger Bacon, as we have seen, would have called the left hemisphere an 'argument' data bank and the right hemisphere an 'experience' data bank. Wagner would have said 'understanding' is stored in the left and 'feeling' in the right hemisphere data bank.

It was, however, an outstanding philosopher of our own time, Abraham H. Maslow, who, as part of his studies of the personality, presented this question in terms so clear that society can no longer ignore the implications for education.

The left hemisphere deals with what Maslow calls 'spectator knowledge.'

> It means looking at something that is not you, not human, not personal, something independent of you the perceiver. It is something to which you are a stranger, a bystander, a member of the audience. You the observer are, then, really alien to it, uncomprehending and without sympathy and identification.[9]

Abraham H. Maslow

9 Abraham H. Maslow, *The Psychology of Science* (Chicago: Henry Regnery, 1966), 49.

What Maslow really means by the term 'spectator knowledge' is that *everything* in the left hemisphere is rational information we have learned as observers, or spectators. Someone tells us, '2 plus 2 equals 4,' or that 'to' is sometimes spelled 'too,' and we file this information away in the left hemisphere, which is the data bank for rational, logical knowledge.

In contrast to this spectator knowledge, Maslow defines the other kind of knowledge as *experiential*, knowledge we arrive at from our own experience. This kind of knowledge is understood by and filed away in our right hemisphere data bank.

To put this in personal terms, everything we *know* in the left hemisphere is information we have been given by someone else and this information we share with everyone else on earth. We are not unique in this knowledge. We agree with everyone on the planet that 2 plus 2 equals 4. No one has a different, personal answer. We spell words the way we have been taught to spell them. All medical students read the same books. In the left hemisphere we are all alike in what we know, varying only in how much of this kind of information we have absorbed.

Quite different is the knowledge of the right hemisphere data bank, the sum of our own personal experience—which, of course, is *unlike* anyone else's experience. It is in this personal, experiential data bank that we are truly *unique*, unlike any other individual on earth.

Consider what we call 'love.' Whatever the word 'love' means to each of us is the sum of our own personal experiences. It is not the sum of everything we have *read* about love. We can read a hundred new books on the subject, they may be interesting and offer new ideas, but they will never change what this word means to *us*, because books can not change our personal experience.

So, which hemisphere is the real us? It really does not take much reflection to see that the *real us* is the experiential, right hemisphere—if by *us* we mean to identify ourselves as individuals. Ornstein agrees:

> It is a constant hope that we're rational and that a judicious component of the human brain controls and orchestrates this parade of talents. Unfortunately for those who hold such a view, but fortunately for the biological survival of the organism, the commanding, controlling mental operating system (which might be called the self) is much more closely linked with emotions and the system of automatic bodyguards than with conscious thought and reason.
>
> …
>
> People look out upon different things in the world, they remember what happened differently, and their reality is actually different … there is no color in nature, no sound, no smell, only movements of waves and molecules. It is we who create the music in the mind, it is we who experience the shift in the composition of gases as perfume.
>
> We build up a world that is different from each other's, individual to individual, culture to culture, species to species.[10]

It is for this reason that all written history has been shaped by the experience and memory of the writer and will never correspond exactly with the true past. The concept of objective history is an impossible one.

It should be no surprise to read, therefore, that John Dickinson of Delaware, addressing the Constitutional Convention in Philadelphia in 1787, warned his colleagues, '*Experience* must be our only guide. *Reason* may mislead us.'[11] Two years earlier, George Washington had written to Lafayette:

> Democratic States must always *feel* before they can see;—it is this that makes their governments slow, but the people will be right at last.[12]

[10] Robert Ornstein, *The Evolution of Consciousness* (New York: Prentice Hall, 1991), 153, 241.

[11] Quoted in Catherine Drinker Bowen, *Miracle at Philadelphia* (Boston: Little, Brown, 1966), 44. Also, Stravinsky once observed, 'Instinct cannot lead you astray; if it does it is not instinct.'

[12] Letter of July 25, 1785, quoted in ibid., 243.

However, because of the ever-present books, pencils, blackboards, and lectures, it turns out that most of the education of Western man is designed only for the left hemisphere. The *real us* is simply not being addressed by the public institutions of education. This was one of the immediate observations by Dr. Roger Sperry, the most important early investigator into the natures of our left and right hemispheres.

> The implications of Sperry's findings ... challenge the priorities of our educational system, which is almost totally geared to the development of the left hemisphere, missing what may be tremendous untapped potentials of the right hemisphere. 'Our educational system and modern society generally discriminate against one whole half of the brain,' says Sperry.[13]

[13] Wayne Sage, 'The Split Brain Lab,' *Human Behavior*, June, 1976.

Another recent philosopher and behavioral scientist, Jean Houston, Director of the Foundation for Mind Research in Pomona, New York, adds,

> A person needs to think in terms of images as well as words. He needs whole-body thinking—to evoke more of his entire mind-body system. Verbal-linear-analytical intelligence is a small part of the intelligence spectrum. There is also visual-aesthetic-plastic (working with the hands) intelligence, but that is not acknowledged in the schools.[14]

[14] Roger M. Williams, 'Why Children Should Draw. The Surprising Link Between Art and Learning,' *Saturday Review*, September 3, 1977.

It is this failure to address the personal, creative side which also disturbs Garrett, who deplored

> the tragic lack of effort to develop our children's right-brain strengths. That potential—a source of equally essential creative, artistic, and intellectual capacity—is at present largely unawakened in our schools.[15]

[15] S. V. Garrett, 'Putting our Whole Brain to Use: A fresh look at the Creative Process,' in *Journal of Creative Behavior*, 1976, 10, 239–249.

A student in Chicago, speaking to the National Commission on Music Education, compared the results of an educational system that only educates half a brain to 'trying to climb a ladder with one leg.'[16]

This tendency toward education of only half the brain has been accelerated in our time by the heavy emphasis on science, as pointed out by Sam Reese.

[16] *Report of the National Commission on Music Education* (Reston: MENC, 1991), 21.

During recent years, Western education has heavily emphasized the intellectual aspects of man almost to the exclusion of emotional, intuitive, and aesthetic experiences. A typical day for an elementary school student includes training in such disciplines as math, social studies, language arts, and science, with perhaps short sessions of music, art, or physical education. This over-emphasis on the intellect has been largely a result of the overwhelming influence of science on modern Western culture.[17]

[17] Sam Reese, 'Discovering the Nonintellectual Self,' *Music Educators Journal*, May 1974.

To which the famous newscaster, Paul Harvey, observed,

Presently we are spending 29 times more on science than on the arts, and the result so far is worldwide intellectual embarrassment.[18]

[18] Paul Harvey, American Broadcasting Company, 1991.

It is interesting that the futility of a science-centered education was apparent to Wagner already in the nineteenth century.

What has Science not pinned its faith to, and not so very long ago, that today lies on the dustheap? The contrary with works of Art; alter, transform your views and sciences as ye will—there still stands Shakespeare, there Goethe's Faust, there the Beethoven Symphony, with undiminished power![19]

[19] William Ashton Ellis, ed., *Wagner's Prose Works* (New York: Broude), VIII, 392.

Maslow argued for a balance between spectator knowledge and experiential knowledge, with the ideal goal that neither become dominant—perhaps he would agree that we should one day give the expression, 'two heads are better than one' a new meaning. He wrote,

In our culture and at this point in history, it is necessary to redress the balance in favor of spontaneity, the ability to be expressive, passive, unwilled, trusting in processes other than will and control, unpremeditated, creative.[20]

[20] Abraham H. Maslow, *Toward a Psychology of Being* (New York: Van Nostrand Reinhold, 1968),198.

It would not be so bad that we educate only half a brain but for the fact that we educate the *wrong* half—the half that is not the real us![21]

[21] There are some very important additional values to right hemisphere education which space makes it impossible to discuss here. I am thinking, for example, of the subject of 'creativity' and also the way in which the right hemisphere connects the student with his environment.

How do We Educate the Rest of Us?

It is the Arts to which we must look to redress the imbalance in our educational institutions. As Maslow concluded,

> If we hope for our children that they will become full human beings and that they will move toward actualizing the potentialities that they have, then, as nearly as I can make out, the only kind of education in existence today that has any kind of faint inkling of such goals is art education.[22]

[22] Abraham H. Maslow, 'The Creative Attitude,' in Avila, et. al., *The Helping Relationship Sourcebook* (Boston: Allyn and Bacon, 1971), 383.

We shall present here some general concepts, and even some specific ones, relative to the education of the right hemisphere of the brain. But first we must always keep in mind that our two hemispheres of the brain are individually quite different in nature. We cannot expect the 'rules' of the right hemisphere to be identical with the 'rules' of the left hemisphere.

To begin with, the right hemisphere seems to have its own unique understanding of formal perception. For example, in listening to a musical composition we find pleasure in recapitulations and da capos, which give us a feeling of 'here we are back home again.' It is a capacity more familiar to us in the form of the pleasure we experience in seeing the face of someone we have not seen for some time, or revisiting a town or place we have known in the past. But there is *nothing* comparable to this in the left hemisphere! The world of numbers start out 1, 2, 3, 4 and *never* returns. And in literature, imagine how ridiculous it would be to read a novel only to find at the end an instruction to go back and *reread* the first five chapters!

Second, I can think of some situations where the left and right hemispheres give *different* answers to the same question, yet with each answer being a *correct* answer from the perspective of the hemisphere involved. Take, for example, the last movement of Mozart's G Minor Symphony (the so-called, 'Nr. 40').

It is a sonata form and the sub-form of the first theme is *AABB*. But in the recapitulation, the form of this theme is *AB*, Mozart obviously shortening it. From the perspective of the left hemisphere, the instructor of a Form and Analysis class might say, 'This is an example of an incomplete recapitulation, as only half of the first theme is present.' Taken as left hemisphere data, that is correct. But the right hemisphere understands the form experientially and has a *completely different* answer. The right hemisphere brings into play a familiar psychological curiosity dealing with the brain's memory archive. Why is it that this hour today seems longer than all of March, 2008, to us? And yet, every hour of every day in March, 2008, was actually as long as the present hour. As things recede in time, they are shortened in the brain's memory of them. Thus what we heard as *AABB* in the exposition section is now remembered by the brain some six minutes later as about half its actual length and thus *AB* now *feels* like a complete and appropriate recapitulation. The right hemisphere says it *is* a complete recapitulation. This same principle, by the way, is why it is important to take the repeats in the exposition sections of sonata forms and the first repeats in minuets.

There are many things one can think of which are somewhat similar to this. Why, for example, can't we hear everything all those tubas play, when we hear everything (too loudly) that the piccolo plays? The scientist, with his decibel machine would say, 'I can prove you are wrong; the tubas *do* produce more sound than the piccolo.' And we would respond, 'I don't care what you say, I can't hear the tubas and the piccolo is too loud!' We have been reared to understand True and False as absolute concepts, but maybe we have been reared to regard only the left hemisphere's version as Truth.

Finally, the right hemisphere's superiority with spatial problems may also give it a much greater precision in problems of time. Every instrumental teacher has struggled with getting young players to play the dotted eighth- sixteenth-note figure so that it doesn't sound like a quarter and eighth-note triplet. At a tempo of MM. quarter-note equals 120, march tempo, we hear an enormous difference between these two rhythms, although the actual difference is measured in hundredths of a second. While this is easy work for the right hemisphere, I am not sure the left hemisphere does anything, or works on any problem, where 'right' or 'wrong' depends on the brain calculating something in that amount of time—it takes quite a bit longer to come up with the answer to 'What is 2 plus 2?' It must surely be this greater ability of the right hemisphere to deal with time in space which makes possible flying state of the art military jet fighters. Some of these planes can move faster than 3,168 feet *per second*. Could the left hemisphere rationalize its way through the problems of flying at that speed?

The feelings and emotions felt in music and emotions and feelings in general are both generally found in the right hemisphere of the brain, which is no surprise because they are both experiential in nature. The left hemisphere of the brain knows the word 'pain' only in an abstract form, that which appears in a dictionary. But in the right hemisphere the word 'pain' has a personal definition based on one's own personal experience with pain. And so it is with words like 'love' and 'music.' Music, therefore, becomes the most approachable means of education in the right hemisphere. Indeed, music is the most powerful means of communication available to the right hemisphere which has no effective 'normal' language.

But here once again we must guard against the left hemisphere, because it owns words and language, distracting us from our purpose. Perhaps our guideposts should be two:

- The left hemisphere is about *thinking*; the right hemisphere about *feeling*.
- Music is for the ear, not the eye.

With these in mind, consider the following two statements:

Music Educators National Conference:
    Music is a form of beauty. It needs no one to justify it.[23]

Distinguished Conductor, Sergiu Celibadache:
    Anyone who still hasn't got past the stage of the beauty of music still knows nothing about music. Music is not beautiful. It has beauty as well, but the beauty is only the bait. Music is true.[24]

The definition of Music which Celibadache has in mind here is discussed in some length by Wagner. Since the Ellis translation of Wagner's German is often stilted, and frequented by poor choices, let me clarify the following points, as they are

[23] *The Report of the National Commission of Music Eduction* (Reston: MENC, 1991), 4.

[24] Quoted in *Los Angeles Philharmonic Notes*, April, 1989.

very important. Wagner says here that [1] Music is the form of communication by the Feeling (experiential) side of us, which can not otherwise speak; [2] Unlike painting, in which we must contemplate a canvas as a prerequisite to finding the 'art,' Music speaks directly to us; [3] Music allows us to 'gaze into the inmost Essence of ourselves; [4] the quality of a composition is determined by the degree to which it helps us do this.

> Music, who speaks to us solely through quickening into articulate life the most universal concept of the inherently speechless Feeling, in all imaginable gradations, can once and for all be judged by nothing but the category of the *sublime*; for, as soon as she engrosses us, she transports us to the highest ecstasy of consciousness of our infinitude. On the other hand what enters only *as a sequel* to our contemplation of a work of plastic art ... the required effect of *beauty* on the mind, is brought about by Music by her very *first entry*; inasmuch as she withdraws us at once from any concern with the relation of things outside us, and—as pure Form set free from Matter—shuts us off from the outer world, as it were, to let us gaze into the inmost Essence of ourselves and all things. Consequently our verdict on any piece of music should be based upon a knowledge of those laws whereby the effect of Beauty, the very first effect of Music's mere appearance, advances the most directly to a revelation of her truest character through the agency of the Sublime. It would be the stamp of an absolutely empty piece of music, on the contrary, that it never got beyond a mere prismatic toying with the effect of its first entry, and consequently kept us bound to the relations presented by Music's outermost side to the world of vision.[25]

[25] Ellis, op. cit., V, 77.

For the performer, Wagner says that it is this 'inmost Essence of ourselves' which is the very seat of his activity.

> An artist addresses himself to Feeling, and not to Understanding. If his work is discussed in terms of Understanding, then it might as well be said he has been misunderstood.[26]

[26] 'Eine Mitteilung an meine Freunde,' 1851.

To which, the great pianist, Alfred Brendel, adds,

> Although I find it necessary and refreshing to *think* about music, I am always conscious of the fact that *feeling* must remain the Alpha and Omega of a musician; therefore my remarks proceed from feeling and return to it.[27]

[27] Quoted in *The New Yorker*, May 30, 1977.

The problem with music education in the United States is that music educators have never had the desire, or the will, or the courage to focus their teaching on the student's experiential self, helping him 'gaze into the inmost Essence' of himself.

We need to *teach* these 'deep human feelings.' We help the student learn this through *music*. I believe the art of teaching music is the art of teaching the student to experience what is beyond the printed page.

The first, and perhaps most vital, step in doing this is to allow the students to experience their own emotions in their experiencing of the music before we begin to conceptualize, talk about it, or analyze it. I am reminded of the old European rule of etiquette regarding one's coming into contact with an aristocrat: 'Don't speak until spoken to.' In other words, we must give the music itself a chance to speak to us, before we begin talking it to death. Thomas Ewens makes this point very well.

> It seems to me that this is a critical issue in art education and one which all parties—artists, art historians, art critics, aestheticians, *and* art educators—should get clear if efforts to reconstruct a viable program of art education are to succeed. Macmurray sees this very clearly. The proper artistic education of the young, he says, is 'a training in perception and expression, which in its full results would develop to the fullest measure of which the child is capable, his ability to be an artist; that is to say, to apprehend the world finely through his own sensibility, and to express it in spontaneous activity purely for the joy in doing so.'[28] Such a training in artistry is not to be based in the three academic disciplines Eisner invokes[29] but in the spontaneous emotional activities, attunements, discernments, appraisals, and imaginary experiments of the child. It is an education geared to making art as a fullness of life for its own sake. Its goal is not to train children's minds in the analysis and understanding of the works of others; its goal is to enable them to see and feel and judge for themselves and to be true to their own emotional experience. We might resume this point in homely terms: just as people, young and old, can enjoy sex and, as the Bible says, 'know' each other without benefit of clergy, so too can they enjoy and know art without benefit of art historians, art critics, and aestheticians.[30]

Dorothy Ling makes the same plea.

> The purpose of artistic experience is to keep open or reopen the doors of perception. It is only through these doors that the channels of creativity, communication, imagination, and affection can operate to

[28] John Macmurray, *Reason and Emotion* (London: Faber and Faber, 1972), 74ff.

[29] Elliot W. Eisner, *The Role of Discipline-Based Art Education in America's Schools* (Los Angeles: The Getty Center for Education, 1978).

[30] Thomas Ewens, 'In Art Education, More DBAE Equals Less Art,' *Design for Arts in Education*, March/April, 1988.

connect us with our innermost selves and with reality. As the maximum intervention of all these channels is indispensable to education, it follows that artistic experience (not information) must be the axis of education ... Access to this experience must be immediate, free from all information, theories, and applied techniques; there is nothing to be taught, only experienced.[31]

[31] Dorothy Ling, *The Original Art of Music* (The Aspen Institute), 66-67.

Of course all music teachers in performance classes have to teach other things, including technique, reading skills, etc. But there are two points I wish to make as clear as possible. When we are teaching technique, sightreading skills, intonation, tone quality, rhythm, dynamics, etc., we are not teaching *music.* We are teaching grammar. Second, no matter how important it is to our end product to talk about these kinds of things in rehearsal, when we do we lose the attention of our students—who are there to make music. You can observe this youself in anyone's rehearsal, from an elementary school to a professional orchestra—watch the faces, and eyes, of the musicians when the conductor begins to talk.

Once again try to remember that you help your cause, and the composer's, immensely by at least allowing the music to make its impression on the students first. I am not talking about simply sightreading 'to see what the music is like.' Rather, I mean creating the environment, and the time, for the students to communicate directly with the music—to allow as much learning as possible to come directly from experiencing the music. An extraordinary example of this goal is mentioned by Wagner, during the period when orchestras were coming to know Beethoven's Ninth Symphony for the first time. The conductor did not explain the work to the players (who were among the best in Europe), he did not analyze it for them, rather he let them learn the music *from the music*—even though it took three years!

> My most thoroughgoing lesson, however, was hearing a performance of that despaired of 'Ninth Symphony' in Paris in the year 1839 played by the so-called Conservatoire orchestra. It was as if scales had fallen from my eyes in regard to its interpretation and I saw at once the secret of the problem's solving. For in every bar the orchestra had learned to recognize the Beethovenian *melody*; which plainly had escaped our brave Leipzig players of that time. The orchestra *sang* that melody.

That was the secret. And it had been laid open by a conductor of no special genius; Habeneck, to whom was due the credit of that great performance, had rehearsed this symphony for one whole winter without feeling anything beyond the impression of its unintelligibleness and ineffectiveness,—an impression as to which it would be difficult to decide whether German conductors have likewise deigned to feel it. Him it moved, however, to rehearse the symphony yet a second and a third year through, and not to rest till the new Beethovenian *melos* had dawned on every member of his orchestra and had been correctly reproduced by each; for these were players of true feeling for melodic phrasing …

The French musician is in so far influenced by the Italian school, to which he primarily belongs, that music to him is unseizable except through Song: to play an instrument well, in his eyes, means to be able to make it sing…. to be able to 'sing' it correctly, however, the *right tempo* had to be found for its every beat, and that was the second point impressed upon my mind on this occasion. Old Habeneck had certainly no abstract aesthetic 'inspiration' of the thing … but *he found the proper tempo, while diligently leading on his orchestra to grasp the symphony's melos.*

But a correct conception of the melos alone can give the proper tempo: the two are indivisible; one conditions the other. And if I do not scruple to declare that by far the most performances of our classic instrumental works are seriously inadequate, I propose to substantiate my verdict by pointing out *that our conductors know nothing of proper Tempo, because of their understanding nothing about Song.* I have never met a single German Kapellmeister or musical conductor who could really *sing* a melody, let his voice be good or bad; no, Music to them is an abstraction, a cross between syntax, arithmetic and gymnastics; so that one may conceive its votaries making fine teachers at a conservatoire or musical gymnasium, but never imagine them breathing life and soul into a musical performance.[32]

Antoine Habeneck

[32] Ellis, op. cit., IV, 300ff.

What this conductor understood must be our real goal for music education: for students to know *music*, not know *about* music. A contemporary philosopher makes the same point in language which should be our credo as music educators.

It is essential to understand here that, for the creator of art and for the appreciator of art, aesthetic experience, enjoyment, and knowledge come *before* all conceptual clarifications, *before* all the learned discourses of art historians, art critics, and aestheticians. As Gilson says, 'The fact that should dominate the discussion is the anteriority of aesthetic experience with respect to any form of discursive knowledge.'[33] One can, of course, transpose the elemental meaning expressed in art into conceptual discourse: this is what art historians, art critics, aestheticians, and others do. However, as Lonergan puts it, 'This procedure reflects with-

[33] Etienne Gilson, *Painting and Reality* (Cleveland: The World Publishing Company, 1961), 218.

out reproducing the elemental meaning. Art criticism and art history are like the thermodynamic equations, which guide our control of heat but, of themselves, cannot make us feel warmer or cooler.'

It also follows from this understanding of art that we must distinguish between enjoying art and learning about it, between knowing art and knowing about it. Aesthetic experience, knowing and enjoying art—the knowing is *in* the enjoying—are prior to and do not depend upon knowing and learning about art. Gilson has some wonderfully pertinent things to say about this in his *Painting and Reality*. He points out, for instance, the dangers of giving students and the general public the impression 'that they do not 'understand' art because they 'know' little or nothing about it.'[34] He repeatedly alerts us to the error of 'letting cognitive activities foreign to its essence invade the art of painting and corrupt its notion in the minds of men.'[35]

To be sure, we may come to want to know as much as we can about art—that, I think, should be a fruit of good early art education—but that desire grows out of our love and delight, out of an aesthetic experience. If students can once taste this in their own work and that of others, then they will be likely to seek more information. Again Gilson: 'All men ultimately desire to know what they love, and find great joy in this kind of knowledge, but in aesthetic experience love comes first.' Now aesthetic experience itself cannot be taught, so whatever is teachable in this area is only indirectly related to aesthetic experience. Eisner, who speaks slightingly of those who think that 'art is caught not taught,' does not seem to recognize the priority and the inviolability of aesthetic experience, nor does he seem to appreciate the implications for art education of the distinction between knowing/loving art and knowing about art; and because he does not he is led to amalgamate art with disciplines 'foreign' to it. Discipline-based art education in his sense denatures art, and one can at least wonder if it would not have the effect of suffocating student interest in art because it would subordinate art to disciplines in which students may as yet have little or no interest because their experience of art itself has been truncated and academicized.[36]

[34] ibid., 102.

[35] ibid., 219.

[36] Ewens, op. cit.

If we fail at this we lose the interest of our students and they begin to identify with Leonard Bernstein's song, 'I Hate Music, but I Love to Sing!' So, if the goal is for the student to both love to sing and love music, we must make sure we are teaching *music* when we teach music.

How do we teach music when we teach music?

We must always begin by remembering that the real music is not on the page.

Felix Weingartner

Gustav Mahler:
   The important things in music are not found in the notes.

Felix Weingartner:
   There are musicians who only see the notes and those who see behind the notes.

Franz Liszt:
   With notes alone nothing can be accomplished; one thirsts for soul, spirit, and actual life.

Bruno Walter:
   The performer's duty is to recreate the spirit of the score, not the letter of the score.

If we are to be effective teachers of music, we must first understand the music before us. The problem is, not all the music is before us. There are two important reasons why no composer has, can or will ever succeed in communicating *all* his musical thought through notation.

First, a page of music is something expressed in a symbolic language just like English. In a symbolic language, including both English and musical notation, the symbols mean *something else*. 'Cat' is not a cat, the letters have nothing to do with cats, but it *represents* a cat. Music notation works just like that: the quarter-notes and half-notes, the C-sharps and B-flats *are not music*. They are a man-made symbolic language which *represents* grammar in music.

Bruno Walter

There is another fundamental problem associated with this first one: we will *never agree* on how to *read* this notation! We can accept the idea of a universal agreement with regard to reading English, because, being a symbolic language of the left hemisphere, it represents concepts upon which there is universal agreement (everyone agrees 2 plus 2 equals 4, etc.). Music notation, however, is a symbolic language which represents 'knowing' in our experiential right hemisphere—where there is no universality, as we are each unique in our experiences. No two musicians ever look at a page and see the same things, and we are forever pointing to a page of Mozart or Beethoven and saying, 'Well, this is what he wrote, but this is not what he meant.'

By the way, it is this inability of the notation to represent *music*, which lies at the heart of explanations of some common characteristics among musicians, the natures of which would be considered most extraordinary in the left hemisphere worlds of science and literature: [1] Why a good musician considers any theory about playing exactly what is on the page to be irrelevant, [2] Why two performers will always create two different versions of the same music (and therefore why we coin the word 'interpreter' so we don't have to try to explain all this to others), and [3] Why it is possible in Music to have fine performing musicians who do not even read music!

If we are to be successful music teachers, we must find all the music which is not on paper. How do we do this?

First, and foremost, we must learn how to absorb music without depending so much on the eye. This could not be more clear than in the problem of notation. The composer begins with an intuitive musical idea, but he can only communicate it to other musicians, and eventually the audience, by turning his intuitive, right hemisphere idea into a left hemisphere language—notation. The performer comes from the other direction. He takes all that is available to him, the left hemisphere notated form of the music, and, using his own experiential right hemisphere data bank, tries to see *beyond* the notation to see what the composer *really* had in mind.

How do we see beyond the notation? The very best way is expressed in an ancient Sufi parable.

> A student was walking through the village, whereupon he came to the house of his teacher. There he saw his teacher, on his hands and knees, apparently looking for something in the grass.
>
> 'Master, what are you looking for?'
>
> 'I am looking for my house key,' his teacher replied, 'Come and help me look for it!'
>
> The student joined his teacher in the grass, but after a time he concluded that there was probably no key in the grass at all and that this was intended as some sort of lesson.
>
> 'OK, Master, where did you actually lose your house key?'
>
> His teacher answered, 'Well, actually I lost it somewhere inside my house.'
>
> 'Why,' said the student, 'are we looking out here in the grass?'
>
> 'Because there is more light here,' reassured the teacher.

The real music will not be found on the page. To find it we must use faculties other than the eye. Since the eye is our most dominant sense, and since the invention of writing (thus, reading) it has evolved so that our mental-visual processing of our field of vision *assumes* that any kind of written language must be fed to the left hemisphere. And, of course, that is quite correct. Musical notation *is* a left hemisphere language. Our hemispheres, fortunately, can work separately but at the same time, so we *can* look at music and at the same time be aware of our feelings. But I believe it is quite a bit more difficult to look at a musical score, which feeds into our left hemisphere, and at the same time contemplate *someone else's* right hemisphere.

This is how the parable helps. If we can get away from the printed score and think about the music experientially, I believe we will be closer to insights into the composer's experience and feelings. By closing the score, we create more light.

Of course, another sense which helps us 'see' more of the music is the ear. We will always hear music quite differently than it appears on paper. Things like texture, or color, and the influence of overtones; the effect of chords heard, rather than seen; the influence of one tone against another, not to mention things like combination tones; these kinds of factors are all quite different 'live' than they are in ink. Hearing the music often reveals what the eye did not see.

The most essential thing to remember about musical notation is that it is only a *symbol* of something else, a symbol of the real thing.[37] This was accurately recognized by the ancient Greeks, who had the earliest music notation we know of. Aristoxenus (b. 379 BC), a student of Aristotle, was careful to make this very point.

> [Just because] a man notes down the Phrygian scale it does not follow that he must know the *essence* of the Phrygian scale. Plainly then notation is not the ultimate limit of our science.[38]

When modern music notation first appeared in Western Europe it is very clear that it was considered to be only a symbolic notation, not an exact one. In fact, Franchino Gaffurio (1451–1518), in his very important music treatise, *Practica Musi-*

[37] Ravel, who suffered from aphasia late in life, was no longer able to express his musical ideas in symbols (musical notation).

[38] Aristoxenus, *The Elements of Harmony*, 16, trans., Henry S. Macran (Hildesheim: Georg Olms Verlag, 1974), 39.

Franchino Gaffurio by Leonardo da Vinci

cae, not only mentions the symbolic nature of notation, but goes further in making the fascinating suggestion that singers were regularly singing things 'which cannot be written down!'

> An interval, or space, can be understood to be the distance between a high and a low sound. Moreover, the mental concept of sound is symbolized in given notes. One must express the fixed, raised and lowered pitches of these notes arranged on a variety of lines and spaces vocally. Consequently, these notes are called vocal symbols. Further, sounds which cannot be written down are committed to memory by usage and practice so that they will not be lost, for their delivery flows imperceptibly into the past.[39]

[39] Irwin Young, trans., *The Practica musicae of Franchinus Gafurius* (Madison: University of Wisconsin Press, 1969), 18.

But there is yet another problem with symbolic languages, alike in both English and music. That is that the symbols inevitably have some limited meaning of their own. An English word, for example, standing by itself has a dictionary meaning. This we might call its universal meaning. But the same word may have a different meaning in common usage, or perhaps according to geography. This we might call a more individualized meaning. Thus, when a speaker uses the word 'cat,' he is using the universal definition, but the listener will usually hear instead an individual definition, reflecting some actual cat he has owned or known. Thus everyone in the audience is actually thinking of a *different* cat, each differing with the image of the speaker!

The same is true for our symbolic language of music. In musical notation we have a very limited, yet universally, agreed upon understanding of, let us say, the difference intended between *piano* and *forte*. On the other hand, we have no agreed upon meaning at all regarding the precise measurement of *piano*. It is simply left to the individual performer's perspective. The development of a symbolic language in both English and music has the advantage of bringing literacy to a broader range of people. The danger is that we will tend to fixate on the symbol and not what it represents experientially.

Thus we have inherited a symbolic musical notation which is incapable of expressing the composer's original, authentic musical ideas, which alone is a significant obstacle to the musician. But in addition to this there is a host of additional, peripheral problems related to musical notation. One is that we can never be quite sure if what we see on paper is what the composer wrote. Here we are not thinking so much of copyist and publisher errors, which are a real enough problem by themselves, but rather the work of that unseen person whose name often never appears on the page, the editor. Here we speak from experience, having once been employed by a major United States publisher as the unseen, anonymous person in the basement who was paid to edit. In one case it was an orchestral score by an important then living composer, to which the unseen person added slurs and articulation markings unknown to the composer. In another case, involving a famous European publishing house, the present writer was paid to prepare an urtext edition of a number of Mozart piano sonatas. But when the present person took the finished manuscripts in to the editor, the editor picked up a pencil and immediately began to draw slurs, change articulations, etc. 'But,' we cried, 'our purpose is to make an urtext edition, just the way Mozart wrote it!' 'Yes,' said the editor, 'but everyone knows this should be slurred.' So a generation of pianists bought an urtext edition which was not really an urtext edition. So can we ever really know what the composer wrote?

Another interesting problem is represented by Verdi, as reported by Toscanini,[40] who believed that no matter what he put on paper, in terms of dynamics, an Italian orchestra would play mezzo-forte at all times. So, in his operas, Verdi would write 'ppp' in the hopes of getting 'p.' Can we ever know what Verdi *really* wanted?

In summary, neither our present notational system, nor any other system of notation that could ever be invented, can precisely communicate, by itself, the composer's original idea. Symbolic language can never be the real thing when it comes to the experiential. Berlioz once wrote,

> It is said that a Greek was once asked to go and hear a man whistle like a nightingale. 'Not I,' replied the Greek, 'I have heard the actual bird.'[41]

The goal, then, is not to teach the students the notes, but the more complete, meaningful, experiential reality the notes represent. Things are made more difficult for us in the fact that we have only one word, Music, which must represent both these concepts. In German, one can see how this is all much more evident to everyone involved, as they have one word, *Die Noten*, for the notes and a different word for the music, *Die Musik*.

Giuseppe Verdi

[40] Related in Erich Leinsdorf, *The Composer's Advocate* (New Haven: Yale University Press, 1981), 200.

[41] 'On Imitation in Music ' (1837).

There is another broad area of musical perception which varies from the page and that is the element of Time. This is a special phenomenon, unique to the world of music. We see Time as a two-dimensional picture on the score page, but we understand it as being in three-dimensions. Once again, we use left hemisphere numbers to describe a right hemisphere spatial understanding. It is yet another example of how we, through conceptualization, transform one thing into something else.

> To insist that music set up patterns against a beat may seem academically narrow and creatively stifling, but a study of Stravinsky's divisions of time should offer persuasive evidence of the importance of these observations. The *Poetics* describes two types of time—the ontological and the psychological. Ontological time is measurable Greenwich mean time by which we set our watches. Music form makes use of it in sensing proportions. Psychological time is the way we measure our emotional reactions to the time involved in events.[42]

[42] Lothar Klein, 'Stravinsky's Poetics: Dialogue of Music and Lifestyle,' *Music Educators Journal*, September, 1973.

The most familiar example of psychological time is something every good musician does frequently, *rubato*. In this case, as Liszt points out, it is often the other elements of music which define the psychological 'correctness' of the meter or rhythm.

> *Rubato* may be left to the taste and momentary feeling of gifted players. A metronomical performance is certainly tiresome and nonsensical; time and rhythm must be adapted to and identified with the melody, the harmony, the accent and the poetry … But how to indicate all this [on paper]? I shudder at the thought of it.[43]

[43] Letter to Siegmund Lebert, January 43 10, 1870.

By the way, I recently read a statement about *rubato* by a very famous living conductor. He claimed that it was an old tradition in music that if one stole time (the literal definition of *rubato*) one must repay it, which he took to mean something in terms of time. First, he is incorrect in his history for what the old writers meant was that if you steal time you must repay the composer by doing something beautiful during that time. As for 'making up time,' somehow we must remember that time does not exist. The entire subject is man-made. There is no time to catch up to.

Wagner commented on his frustration with the conductors of the smaller opera houses in Germany, often conductors of the local church or regimental military band, who tended to perform exactly what was on the page, thus rendering the music in a very mechanical nature.

> I furnished my earlier operas—those played at the theaters—with downright eloquent directions for tempo, and fixed them past mistaking (so I thought) by metronomic numbers. But whenever I heard of a foolish tempo in a performance of my 'Tannhauser,' for example, my recriminations were always answered by the pleas that my metronomic marks had been followed most scrupulously. So I saw how uncertain must be the value of mathematics in music, and thenceforth dispensed with the metronome …
>
> To be sure, I am speaking of the thorough bunglers, people who have an uncommon dread of the *alla breve* beat and always abide by four strictly measured quarter-strokes per bar, apparently to keep awake their consciousness that they're conducting to some purpose. How these four-footed creatures ever jumped from their village churches to our opera houses, God only knows.[44]

[44] 'On Conducting,' quoted in William Ashton Ellis, ed., *Wagner's Prose Works* (New York: Broude), IV, 304.

Another good example of psychological time is Placement, by which is meant beginning a new phrase, after a cadence, when it *feels* correct to begin, as opposed to what is indicated in mathematical time (notation).

There are also important characteristics of the environment in which we hear music which have psychological influences on how we hear time. For example, Eugene Ormandy once told me that he purposely recorded slow movements faster than he would perform them live, because he believed the listener, distracted by the activities of his home, could not maintain the concentration necessary for slow tempi.

Tempo is another fundamental of music in which there is a danger that we present a left hemisphere understanding to the student. What Dalcroze once wrote is very true:

> How is it that the rubato style adopted by most pianists is generally regarded as a favorable proof of sensibility, whereas it would not be tolerated for a moment in an orchestral performance?[45]

[45] Emile Jaques-Dalcroze, 'Contradictions and Inconsistencies' (1922), in *Eurhythmics, Art and Education* (New York: Sarnes, 1931), 252.

It is certainly true today that conductors are generally much more reserved than individual artists with regard to modification of tempo within a movement. But it was not always so.

Gunther Schuller, in his conducting book, could not be more misinformed when he suggests that Baroque music was so 'steady' that no conductor was needed.[46] Following are some observations, taken from many, by Baroque musicians which reflect much more freedom than performers today would dare.

In 1615, Frescobaldi wrote,

> These pieces should not be played to a strict beat any more than modern madrigals which, though difficult, are made easier by taking the beat now slower, now faster, and by even pausing altogether in accordance with the expression and meaning of the text.[47]

Giovanni Bonachelli, in 1642, also suggested that feeling is the key.

> In accordance with the feeling one must guide the beat, sensing it now fast, now slow, according to the occasion, now liveliness, and now languor, as indeed anyone will easily know immediately who possesses the fine manner of singing.[48]

Thomas Mace, in 1676, seems to suggest that the freedom in time extended even to form! If, he says, the music falls into sections, these may be played,

> according as they best please your own fancy, some very briskly, and courageously, and some again gently, lovingly, tenderly and smoothly.
> …
> Beginners must learn strict time; but when we come to be masters, so that we can command all manner of time, at our own pleasures; we then take liberty … to break time; sometimes faster and sometimes slower, as we perceive, the nature of the thing requires.[49]

During the nineteenth century we still find the same ideals expressed. Weber, in a letter to the music director, Praeger in Leipzig, wrote of the importance of tempo modification.

> The beat must not be like a tyrannical hammer, impeding or urging on, but must be to the music what the pulse-beat is to the life of man.
> There is no slow tempo in which passages do not occur that demand a quicker motion, so as to obviate the impression of dragging.
> Conversely there is no presto that does not need a quiet delivery in many places, so as not to throw away the chance of expressiveness by hurrying …

[46] Gunther Schuller, *The Compleat Conductor* (Oxford: Oxford University Press, 1997), 71. On the following page, Schuller is also misinformed regarding the usage of 'measure' and 'movement' during the Baroque. 'Movement' meant character, or moving the emotions, not tempo as he says. This is so clear in Baroque sources we are quite puzzled that he misunderstood this.

[47] Girolamo Frescobaldi (1583-1643), *Toccatas and Partitas*, Book I.

[48] Giovanni Bonachelli, *Corona di sacri gigli a una, due, tre, quattro, e cinque voci* (Venice, 1642), preface.

[49] Thomas Mace, *Musick's Monument* [1676] (Paris: Éditions du Centre National de la Recherche Scientifique, 1966), 429, 432.

Carl Maria von Weber

> Neither the quickening nor the slowing of the tempo should ever give the impression of the spasmodic or the violent. The changes, to have a musical-poetic significance, must come in an orderly way in periods and phrases, conditioned by the varying warmth of the expression.[50]

Wagner complained that the 'conductor-guild' of his time held that there should be no tempo modification in the music of Beethoven, a view which Wagner attributes to 'the incapacity and general unfitness of our conductors themselves.' He hastens to add that he does not mean 'the willful introduction of random nuances of tempo.'[51]

When Brahms conducted his Fourth Symphony with the famous Meiningen Orchestra he had difficulty achieving fully expressive performances and afterward wrote Joseph Joachim saying (of things not notated in the score) 'In these concerts I couldn't make enough slowings and accelerations.'[52]

If it is true that we modern musicians are somewhat conservative about tempi modification, we are terrified when we see a metronome marking.[53] These metronome numbers are taken as direct commandments from the composer and we dare not depart from the number given! But once again, the view of our earlier colleagues was quite different. They seem to have regarded the metronome marking as only a suggestion for the first few bars. Beethoven, for example, wrote on one of his autograph scores,

> 100 according to Maelzel; but this must be held applicable to only the first measures, for feeling also has its tempo and this cannot entirely be expressed in this figure.[54]

And Berlioz, in his essay on conducting:

> I do not mean to say that it is necessary to imitate the mathematical regularity of the metronome, which would give the music thus executed an icy frigidity; I even doubt whether it would be possible to maintain this rigid uniformity for more than a few bars.

And Brahms, as he attempts to answer a nervous conductor:

> I hardly know what to answer: 'If the indications by figures of the tempi in my Requiem should be strictly adhered to?' Well—just as with all other music. I think ... that the metronome is of no value ... The so-called 'elastic' tempo is moreover not a new invention.[55]

---

[50] Quoted in Felix Weingartner, *On Conducting* (New York: Kalmus), 41.

[51] Wagner's Prose Works, op. cit., IV, 336. H. A. VanderCook's book, *Expression in Music* (Chicago: Rubank, 1926), 42, gives an illustration of four bars of music with a different written tempo in each bar (quarter-note 60, 72, 66 and 60 respectively). Doing this sort of thing, he recommends, will eliminate 'humdrum results.'

[52] *Johannes Brahms im Briefwechsel mit Joseph Joachim* (Berlin, 1908), II, 205.

[53] William Finn, in *The Conductor Raises his Baton* (London: Dobson, 1944), 84, recommends rehearsing with an amplified metronome so as to induce confidence in the musicians! We have seen a Texas band director use a makeshift device combining a metronome and a highway safety light blasting metronomic beams of light into his young musicians' consciousness.

[54] Quoted in Erich Leinsdorf, *The Composer's Advocate* (New Haven: Yale University Press, 1981), 165.

[55] ibid., 129.

And Verdi, in a note in his *Te Deum:*

> This entire piece ought to be performed in one tempo as indicated by the metronome. This notwithstanding, it will be appropriate to broaden or accelerate in certain spots for reasons of expression and nuance.[56]

And Wagner, writing of performance suggestions for *Tannhäuser*:

> As to the 'tempi' of the whole work in general, I here can only say that if conductor and singers are to depend for their time-measure on the metronomical marks alone, the spirit of the work must stand indeed in sorry case.[57]

Among conductors, Bruno Walter also suggests that the Metronome marking is good only 'for the first few bars, but must needs lose its validity as soon as a change in expression demands a modification of speed.'[58] Erich Leinsdorf pretty much brings the discussion to a close: 'I do not consult the little clock.'[59]

Probably the best advice to musicians regarding tempi is Beethoven's: 'feeling has its tempo.' Monteverdi made the same observation in his *Madrigali guerrieri et amorosi* (Venice, 1638) when he spoke of the voice following 'her lament, which is sung to the time of the heart's feeling, and not to that of the hand.' Once again, feeling, and not mathematics, is the key.[60]

As the musician must permit his heart to overrule metronomic markings, so he must allow his heart to translate the familiar Italian tempo terms as they are found in specific compositions. Most musicians today think of these familiar Italian words in terms of rather specific tempi, but earlier musicians associated them with the *character* of the music. The views of these earlier writers can seem rather extraordinary today, for example when Johann Mattheson (1681–1764) writes,

> An *Adagio* indicates distress; a *Lamento* lamentation; a *Lento* relief; an *Andante* hope; an *Affetuoso* love; an *Allegro* comfort; a *Presto* eagerness.[61]

[56] ibid., 130.

[57] *Prose Works of Wagner*, op. cit., III, 190.

[58] Walter, op. cit., 43.

[59] Leinsdorf, op. cit., 130.

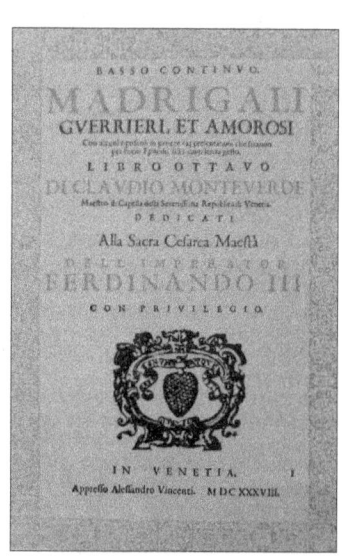

Monteverdi's Madrigali guerrieri et amorosi *(Venice, 1638)*

[60] Some anomalies: Von Karajan, in Richard Osborne, *Conversations with Von Karajan* (New York: Harper & Row, 1989), 101, says slow music with intermittent pauses puts such stress on the system as can cause death! He was thinking in particular of two conductors who died while conducting Act III of Tristan. The famed choral conductor, William Finn, in op. cit., 62ff, presents a curious discussion on racial aspects of tempo. He finds, for example, that the Nordic character is to be associated with a slower tempo than the Latins.

[61] Johann Mattheson, *Der vollkommene Capellmeister* (1739), trans., Ernest Harris (Ann Arbor: UMI Research Press, 1981), II, xii, 34ff.

And Roger North (1653–1734):

> The *Grave* comes nearer a sober conversation, and the *Allegro* light and chirping. The *Tremolo* is fear and suspicion, the *Andante* is a walking about full of concern, the *Ricercata* is a searching about for somewhat out of the way; the *Affectuoso* is expostulating, or *amour*; and so every other manner, as masters are pleased to title them, are but so many states of humane life, as they have a fancy to represent or imitate.[62]

[62] Quoted in John Wilson, *Roger North on Music* (London: Novello, 1959), 119ff.

Perhaps the single most common error with regard to tempo in earlier music, is the interpretation of the 'Andante' in Mozart, which is usually heard entirely too slow. Even Georg Solti admits he had trouble with this.

> Gradually, however, I found my way. I began to understand that 'andante' means 'moving at a natural tempo,' not 'slow,' and that Mozart must never be heavy or slow.[63]

[63] Sir Georg Solti, *Memoirs* (New York: Alfred Knopf, 1997), 212.

Consider, for example, the etheral *Ave, verum corpus*, a work one would automatically think of as a 'slow' piece. It is even marked 'Adagio,' but choirs sing it at a natural tempo of about M.M. half-note = 72 (quarter-note = 144!).[64]

Today only a few of the traditional terms, such as *Grave*, still carry an implication of character as well as speed. But in performing earlier music, one should trust the ear and not the eye.

[64] This famous work was written at the same time, and has the same emotional character as the 'slow' movement of the Clarinet Concerto, which is also marked Adagio, and which all clarinetists drag along at a lugubrious M.M. = 60, or even less. If they would listen to the orchestral accompaniment, limping along very strangely, instead of listening to their teacher, they would alter the tempo immediately.

Teaching Fundamentals in an Experiential (Right Hemisphere) Mode

As music teachers we must teach all the fundamentals of music, but we must make an effort to find ways to do this which do not close off the student's perception of the *rest* of music. To this end, we need to block, as much as possible, the left hemisphere, for the two hemisphere's have different agenda (I am reminded of the old popular song, 'Your lips say "No," but your eyes say "Yes"').

The first danger is language itself, since it has a tendency toward the left hemisphere. Technical language is even worse, as being of the impersonal left hemisphere, it also sounds negative: 'You are flat!' But we can speak using imagery, poetic, or emotional language to describe musical ideas to our students and I think this helps. One example I use (borrowed from Solti) is the expression, 'Pom Pom,' to describe two chords, to be played warmly, with a slight space.

Most important, in this regard, is the *singing* voice. The singing voice *is* a voice of the right hemisphere! Thus we can sing a complex rhythm, for example, and the students immediately understand it and can play it back—whereas if we expressed it in mathematical terms, it would take forever and the students probably would not listen closely enough to absorb it. When I was a young music education student, I was told *never* to sing in rehearsal! If you can not put it into words, the reasoning went, you do not understand it. How wrong this is!

Teaching Rhythm

Rhythm is taught as mathematics. The origin of this tradition clearly lies in the late medieval universities when all music courses were under the mathematics faculty and all music instruction was given by mathematicians. It is no wonder that as modern European notation was developed, the first concern, after pitch, was rhythm and meter. The 'beats' became the 'numbers' needed for a mathematical explanation of time in music, as is evident in the proportional 'meters' expressed by fractions. It was to establish a mathematical definition of 'one' that theorists such as Gafurius began associating the 'beat' with the human pulse as the basic unit of time.[65] This, of course, makes no sense if one considers the wide variety of pulse rates which fall into the 'normal' range, not to mention the extreme fluctuation of pulse due to emotional factors. And if matters of time are considered primarily as mathematics, then it follows that the only aesthetic judgment that can apply is *correctness*, the same as in mathematics. Thus in Shakespeare's *Richard II*, following a stage direction reading, 'The music plays,' the king observes,

> Music do I hear?
> Ha, ha! Keep time. How sour sweet music is
> When time is broke and no proportion kept![66]

[65] See Irwin Young, trans., *The Practica musicae of Franchinus Gafurius* (Madison: University of Wisconsin Press, 1969), 69.

[66] *Richard II*, act 5, scene 5, line 41ff.

In our view any association of mathematics with music is in fundamental conflict with the paramount purpose of music, which is to communicate feeling. Nevertheless, some musicians, even distinguished musicians, think about mathematics. It is amazing to us to read Bruno Walter's emphasis on mathematics in this regard. He finds the origin of rhythm in such things as the pulse of dancing feet and the two-part pulse of the *arsis* and *thesis* of Greek poetry. He writes a measure of 9/8, converts it into arithmetic proportions and then concludes,

> As one can see, these are uncomplicated relations between note-values which, without any effort at mathematical speculation, can be immediately perceived by anyone with a normal head for figures and sense of time.[67]

[67] Bruno Walter, *Of Music and Music-Making* (New York: Norton, 1957), 45ff.

We are astonished to find so distinguished a musician, whose own performances never exhibited such academic thinking, maintaining that the purpose of rhythm was neither movement, nor feeling, but merely the beats.

> The rhythmic life of music, then, consists in the alternation of long and short, heavy and light, tenuto and staccato, and the rhythmic task of the executant lies in the appropriate gradation of these elements, and their accordance with the melodic–harmonic content of the musical phrases.

One can understand this point of view in the context of the early universities where music was only conceptual, something on paper. But in real music, music heard live, rhythm exists in a state of movement through time and space. We suspect such an association of time with movement was widely understood before modern notation, especially when one recalls the emphasis given movement by the ancient Greek choruses and the sequential understanding of rhythm based on Greek poetry. In fact, the very word 'rhythm' has as its root the Greek *rhythmos*, from *rheo*, meaning *to flow*!

Martianus Capella, in the fifth century for example, made an important observation when he defined 'a tone' as something 'stretched over a space.'[68] It is also significant that he recognized that rhythm can be 'visual' as well as aural. All rhythm, he says, falls into three categories: visual, auditory, or tactual.

[68] *Martianus Capella and the Seven Liberal Arts*, trans., William Harris Stahl and Richard Johnson (New York: Columbia University Press, 1977), II, 370.

An example of the visual is in bodily movements; of auditory, in an appraisal of a vocal performance; of tactual, when a doctor looks for symptoms by feeling the pulse.⁶⁹

[69] ibid., 373.

Wagner addressed this idea of time having to do with space in his discussion of drama.⁷⁰ He points out that the words 'Time' and 'Space' are intellectual concepts representing real physical phenomena. But, he says, the minute you *think* about them they have already lost their meaning, for the true meaning can only be understood in *actual* motion through space.

[70] William Ashton Ellis, *Wagner's Prose Works* (New York: Broude), II, 349ff.

Emile Jaques-Dalcroze, whose system of music education begins with movement, often wrote of the relationship of rhythm and movement. In an article published in 1907, he explains,

> Muscles were made for movement, and rhythm is movement. It is impossible to conceive a rhythm without thinking of a body in motion. To move, a body requires a quantum of space and a quantum of time. The beginning and end of the movements determine the amount of time and space involved.⁷¹

Emile Jaques-Dalcroze

[71] Dalcroze, 'The Initiation into Rhythm,' in *Rhythm Music & Education* (London: Dalcroze Society, 1980), 39.

In the same article he speaks of the personal relationship of the conductor with rhythm and movement.

> Observe the movements by which a conductor of an orchestra, endowed with temperament, represents and transmits rhythm … His whole body will be seen to co-operate in his representation of the rhythm: each articulation, each muscle, contribution to render the rhythmic impression more intense; the aspect of his whole person becoming, in short, the reflected image of the movement of the music, and animating the executants—his own representation of the rhythm being transmitted to them.⁷²

[72] ibid., 42.

We believe von Karajan was perhaps thinking of time as space, rather than as beats, when he observed,

> What you should know is how much tempo passes *overall* in one certain phrase, and this is the most important thing.⁷³

[73] Richard Osborne, *Conversations with Von Karajan* (New York: Harper & Row, 1989), 100.

One eyewitness reports that Mahler, in particular, personified the *movement* of time, rather than thinking of beats as mathematical arrival points.

Conducting, according to Mahler, should be a continual elimination of the bar, so that it retreats behind the melodic and rhythmic content ... On the contrary, the average plodding conductor treats every bar-line as a barrier, and scans the subdivisions of each measure indiscriminately ...

In Mahler's conducting, it is often impossible to distinguish what beat he is using. His baton strokes serve only to emphasize the significant melodic and rhythmic content at any one moment. Consequently, he often guides completely over the first beat of a bar, and stresses instead the second or third beat, or wherever the principal emphasis should be placed.[74]

Although we regard movement the essence of rhythm and time in music, we cannot ignore a relationship with the emotions.[75] Walter wrote about this briefly, but he had it all wrong. He suggests that feeling is an *addition* of 'energy' by the conductor, not a characteristic found in the rhythm itself. A better explanation relates to life, as Jaques-Dalcroze explains:

> Rhythm is to intuition, emotion, and aesthetics what scientific order and logic are to the intellect. One of the essential qualities—if not the essential quality—of rhythm is its power of conveying the presence of life.[76]

Here are additional observations by Jaques-Dalcroze on the subject of rhythm and emotions which might be of special interest to musicians.[77]

> The aim of eurhythmics is to enable pupils, at the end of their course, to say, not 'I know,' but 'I have experienced,' and so to create in them the desire to express themselves; for the deep impression of an emotion inspires a longing to communicate it, to the extent of one's powers, to others.
>
> ...
>
> Rhythm is the live essence of feeling, the fundamental impulse of a movement in the form impressed on it by the first emotional reaction.
>
> ...
>
> Gesture must define musical emotion and call up its image.
>
> ...
>
> Gesture itself is nothing—its whole value depends on the emotion that inspires it.

[74] Natalie Bauer-Lechner, *Recollections of Gustav Mahler*, ed., Peter Franklin, trans., Dika Newlin (Cambridge: Cambridge University Press, 1980), 109.

[75] Note the close relationship of the words themselves: Motion—Emotion. Aristides Quintilianus, who lived between the first and fourth century, A.D., was a philosopher who believed you could determine a man's character by the rhythm of his walk.

> We find that people whose steps are of good length and equal, in the manner of the spondee, are stable and manly in character: those whose steps are long but unequal, in the manner of trochees or paions, are excessively passionate: those whose steps are equal but too short, in the manner of the pyrrhic, are spineless and lack nobility: while those whose steps are short and unequal, and approach rhythmical irrationality, are utterly dissipated. As to those who employ all the gaits in no particular order, you will realize that their minds are unstable and erratic.

[SEE Andrew Barker, *Greek Musical Writings* (Cambridge: Cambridge University Press, 1989), II, 457ff.]

[76] Jaques-Dalcroze, quoting James Shelly's 'Rhythm and Arts,' in 'Rhythm, Time, and Temperament (1919) op. cit., 186.

[77] ibid., 63, 107, 119, 139.

When we teach the elements of music, I believe it helps to teach them holistically, and not through abstraction. For example, how often has it been our experience to write a rhythm on the blackboard, and explain it thoroughly, only to wonder once again why our students don't *feel* rhythm. But if we want our students to *feel* rhythm, why do we abstract it in this way, teaching it as a separate, intellectual piece of left hemisphere data?

I also believe it is important to stay in the character of the music, when dealing with fundamentals in rehearsal. I remind my conducting students that in rehearsal there are three forms of the score present. One is the score on the conductor's stand, which, as we have seen above, is of limited help as it is incomplete. Another form of the score is the one being played, the one we hear in rehearsal—which may be something quite different from the one on the conductor's stand! The third score is the one in the conductor's head, hopefully the most complete and correct one. I encourage young conductors to listen to that score and ignore, in so far as possible, the other two. By that I mean, when listening to that sensitive, beautiful passage in your head, it seems wrong to me to suddenly rage in anger at the version of this passage in the room.

As a means of reaching the right hemisphere of the student, I also place great emphasis on allowing the individual student to contribute to the interpretation. This seems very reasonable to me since the goal is not to play what's on paper anyway. Also, as Mahler points out, each piece of music will be heard differently by each student, and differently yet again tomorrow.

> But the chief thing is still the artistic conception, which no mere words can ever explain. Its truth shows a different face to each one of us—and a different one to each of us at different ages; just as Beethoven's symphonies are new and different at every hearing and never the same to one person as to another.[78]

This reminds me of an occasion some years ago when for a week I observed Loren Maazel rehearsing a Beethoven Symphony with the Philadelphia Orchestra. Then, the orchestra made a weekend tour to New York and Boston. When I heard their performance in Philadelphia on the following Monday, I was astonished to hear that the interpretation had changed

[78] Quoted in, Alma Mahler, *Gustav Mahler* (New York: Viking Press, 1969), 320.

noticeably, even down to articulations. When I asked Loren what had happened to the interpretation over the weekend, he responded, 'I don't know, it just took on a life of its own!'

Of course, the fact that each musician hears music differently, because of our experiential uniqueness, requires of us great tolerance. One interpretation will always seems right to us, and another wrong. Wagner gives an interesting example of this from his own experience.

Loren Maazel

79 Quoted in William Ashton Ellis, ed., *Wagner's Prose Works* (New York: Bourde), IV, 344.

> At a time when I came into contact with a young musician who had been in Mendelssohn's company, I was perpetually told of the master's one piece of advice: In composing never think of making a sensation or effect, and avoid everything likely to lead to it. That sounded beautiful and right enough, and in fact not a single faithful pupil of the master's has ever chanced to produce a sensation or effect … I imagine all the teachings of the Leipzig Conservatory are founded on that negative maxim, for I have heard that the young folk there are plagued to death with its warning, whilst the most promising talents can gain them no favor with their teachers unless they forswear all taste for music not in strict accordance with the Psalms …
>
> Once I begged one of the most reputed older musicians and comrades of Mendelssohn to play me the Eighth Prelude and Fugue from the first part of the Well-tempered Klavier, as that piece had always had such a magical attraction for me; I must admit that seldom have I felt so great a shock as that experienced from his friendly compliance. At any rate there then was no question of gloomy German Gothic…under the hands of my friend the piece flowed over the keyboard with such a 'Grecian gaiety' … that involuntarily I saw myself seated in a neo-Hellenic synagogue, from whose musical rites every trace of the Old Testament accentuation had been decently purged away. That singular reading was still ringing in my ears, when one day I begged Liszt to cleanse my musical feelings from the painful impression. He played for me the Fourth Prelude and Fugue. Now, I knew what to expect from Liszt at the pianoforte … but I never expected what I learnt that day. For then I saw the difference between study and revelation; through his rendering of this single fugue Liszt revealed the whole of Bach to me, so that I now know of a surety where I am with him, can take his every bearing from this point, and conquer all perplexity and every doubt by power of strong faith.[79]

As an example of how I invite student participation in interpretation, if I am conducting a large honor band, and a large clarinet or flute section has a long melody which needs shaping, I will say, 'Just interpret this however you *feel* it; add crescendi, decrescendi, melodic accents, whatever you feel, but turn this line into a melody.' The invariable result is that the students will genetically do all the same things that I would have taken twenty minutes to do by having them mark this and that detail (in left hemisphere language) with their pencils.

On many occasions in conducting I have told a group something like, 'I don't hear any pain.' The change which one hears the next time they play that passage is extraordinarily vivid.

The goal is to try to engage the feeling side of the student, and not just the intellectual side.

If we can learn to teach the *real* child and to teach music as a right hemisphere language through which the individual student learns about himself, his feelings and his emotions, society will come to appreciate our discipline. Society will come to understand,

- that it is music teachers, not philosophy teachers, who can help students discover their real self

- that it is music teachers, not English teachers, who can help students communicate their feelings

- that it is music teachers, not science teachers, who help students connect their *own* experiences and feelings with their environment

- that it is music teachers, not history teachers, who can help students associate earlier periods of time *with themselves*

- that English grammar teachers teach students to speak alike, while music teachers teach students to express themselves as individuals

- that Foreign language teachers teach students the language of another country, while music teachers share a language spoken by all peoples.

These are not examples of how music *helps* other courses. These are examples of things music can teach, which other courses can not.

Music education which is experience based, and not concept based, which is a language of the feelings, and not a skill, can produce an adult who understands and can communicate their own feelings, who is a balanced and more holistic person, who will be capable of participating in the world as an *individual* acting on the basis of their experience rather than acting on the basis of learned responses, and who will continue to use what they learned the rest of their life. What other 'core subject' could claim as much?

7 *Two Paramount New Purposes*

ANY OBJECTIVE PERSON looking at the declining enrollment figures for public school music education for the past fifty years must wonder how long this tradition will last. In a coming era of growing population and shrinking financial resources there will be more and more questions about the value to the school and to society of these costly music programs. The public will want to know what it is that we do that pays society back. Certainly the public will demand more than out-of-school activities and certainly more than providing entertainment activities for a public already saturated with entertainment.

Music educators are going to have to be prepared to explain what it is we do that no other subject in the public school can do. In the previous chapters we have pointed to our advantage in educating the right hemisphere of the brain—the half virtually ignored by traditional education.

But there are two other vital areas in child formation where music teachers can, and in our view must, make a contribution to society. If we can develop teaching strategies and materials in these two areas they may possibly turn out to be that which leads society to conclude that we are indispensable in the curriculum.

Martin Luther

The First Paramount New Purpose: Enabling Students to Discover their 'Other' Self, their Emotional Template

> Only music deserves being extolled as the mistress and governess of the feelings of the human heart.
> Martin Luther (1538)

Music is the shortest way to expressing how little music has to do with the notes. The notes are physical, coarse textured phenomena. But in its relationship to another note, a note can become something which finds an echo in the human emotions. The reasons for this can be experienced in phenomenology, and demonstrated wonderfully. If it weren't for this relationship between the physical phenomenon of sound and the emo-

Sergiu Celibidache

[1] Sergiu Celibidache, quoted in *Los Angeles Philharmonic Notes*, April, 1989.

tional reaction, no one would want to make music, no one would have any interest in it. But it wakens something in us, and we sing and play to liberate ourselves again through this responsiveness.[1]
    Sergiu Celibidache (1989)

The above propositions, by a famous preacher and a famous conductor separated by four hundred and fifty years, echo one of the oldest inscriptions of the Greek language, found amid the ruins of a Delphi Temple:

Know Thyself!

The Temple to Apollo, Delphi

Physiologically speaking, there is only one way to 'know thyself' and that is finding a route for self-discovery within the right hemisphere of one's brain. Everything stored in the left hemisphere is someone else, information you were told or read of regarding passed down information. But the right hemisphere consists exclusively of your own experiential world, what has been passed down to you genetically and what you have experienced and have learned from that experience.

However, while your right hemisphere is the real you, getting to 'know thyself' is difficult because the right hemisphere has no language. It is mute and cannot speak.[2] Its most effective form of communication is music, for the basic role of music is to communicate the emotions, which like the experiential aspects of music is also based in the right hemisphere.

[2] The right hemisphere contains some vocabulary from the first few years before the final connection of the corpus callosum, but it cannot make sentences with that vocabulary.

This has roots in the earliest chapter of man and for a very long time scholars and philosophers have understood the close connection of emotions and music.³

For many centuries philosophers, particularly Church philosophers, argued, 'Reason must Rule!' The very fact that they continued, century after century, to cry this suggests the public was not paying any attention. And the public was correct in ignoring this credo because their common practice suggested what has now been proven in clinical studies: in matters of daily life we do not make decisions on the basis of Reason; we make emotional decisions. What car to buy, what house to buy, which spouse to marry, what to eat for dinner, which movie to see—these are all exclusively emotional decisions— right hemisphere decisions (the *real us!*) and no amount of left brain data has much influence. The student will get no advice from the school room for, among other problems, the teacher is afraid to bring up the subject of the emotions.

The role of the emotions in decision making is emphasized by Robert Ornstein, in his book on the evolution of the mind:

> Many individuals also distrust emotions, seeing them as disruptive, against 'our' interest. They disorganize us, confuse us, lead us astray, or make us irrational: 'If you thought about it, you'd see that you shouldn't marry him or her; move to India; run away from home; panic and bolt.' Or should you?
>
> Emotions rarely disorganize thought to the person's detriment, and disorganization isn't always a plight. When an organized situation such as a job or a marriage isn't working, the surrendering organization is adaptive. The worry that emotions are disorganizing is wrong, anyway, indeed, they are the chief *organizing* system of the mind.
>
> Outside consciousness, emotions, direct the mind toward particular conclusions. They are mind systems adapted to short-circuit deliberation, to making the correct response in life-and-death situations, when fitness is paramount.
>
> Immediate feelings highlight events, sending the rest of the mind a message that something important is happening. An animal that becomes fearful and excited about an approaching attacker is readier to respond and to defend itself. A human who experiences sexual love is more likely to reproduce than one who does not. An enraged organism is prepared to attack; a fearful one is prepared, immediately, to flee. They, like all our reactions, aren't always correct in all situations, but on the average emotions mesh us with the world.

³ For a book which recalls many curious variations in real patients we recommend highly [Dr.] Oliver Sacks, *Musicophilia, Tales of Music and the Brain* (New York: Knopf, 2007).

Emotions come to the fore when rationality is maladaptive. You don't have time to decide whether some food you're eating is slightly spoiled or in fact is poisonous. You could test it yourself or feed it to ten other people in a nice little rational investigation. But then you might be dead. So you make a face and throw it out or throw it up. Sometimes, of course, your reaction might be incorrect—the food might be fine, but how could you know in time? And would it be worth the risk? We remember, think, and feel every day because of the way our mental processes were organized.[4]

[4] Robert Ornstein, *The Evolution of Consciousness* (New York: Prentice Hall, 1991), 87ff.

And, by the way, there is a curious aspect of this with regard to how we identify with our professions. It is not the accumulation of spectator data in the left hemisphere that defines who we are, it only defines, at best, what we do, our career field. It is this accumulation of data that makes us either a lawyer or an insurance salesman. But when an insurance salesman thinks, silently, to himself, 'who am I?' is that answer—'insurance salesman'? For most people the answer is 'no.' Many people, in fact, identify with their hobbies, rather than their profession. They say, 'My job is selling insurance, but cooking is what I love.' Or, 'I grow roses,' or 'I play banjo.' But, nobody's hobby is selling insurance!

As we have mentioned above, language, being left hemisphere, is of very little value in communicating the emotional side of ourselves. But music can do this, as numerous people have observed. A sampling:

> Language is not subtle enough, tender enough to express all we feel, and when language fails, the highest and deepest longings are translated into music.
> Robert Ingersoll

> Where words fail, music speaks.
> Hans Christian Anderson

> There is so much talk about music, and yet so little is said. For my part, I believe that words do not suffice for such a purpose, and if I found they did suffice I would finally have nothing more to do with music.
> Mendelssohn

> Music is a means of communicating with people, not an aim in itself.
> Moussorgsky

Language is one of our most important forms of communication, but anyone who has tried to write a love letter knows that language is quite inferior in the realm of the expression of emotions. Furthermore, when it comes to our most sensitive feelings we often don't want to talk about them at all! Here language fails us.

> Everybody knows that language is a very poor medium for expressing our emotional nature. It merely names certain vaguely and crudely conceived states, but fails miserably in any attempt to convey the ever-moving patterns, the ambivalences and intricacies of inner experience, the interplay of feelings with thoughts and impressions, memories and echoes of memories, transient fantasy, or its mere runic traces, all turned into nameless, emotional stuff. If we say that we understand someone else's feeling in a certain matter, we mean that we understand why he should be sad or happy, excited or indifferent, in a general way; that we can see due cause for his attitude. We do not mean that we have insight into the actual flow and balance of his feelings, into that 'character' which 'may be taken as an index of the mind's grasp of its object.' Language is quite inadequate to articulate such a conception. Probably we would not impart our actual inmost feelings even if they could be spoken. We rarely speak in detail of entirely personal things.[5]

[5] Susanne K. Langer, *Philosophy in a New Key* (New York: Mentor Books, 1948), 92.

In another place, Langer concludes,

> Language and music are similar in that both are means for expressing something. The difference is that language is principally a means for expressing ideas, and music is principally a means for expressing feelings.[6]

[6] Susanne K. Langer, 'The Cultural Importance of the Arts,' *The Journal of Aesthetic Education*, Spring 1966, 5-12.

That most rational of left hemisphere language, science, is also of little value in the communication of emotions. Science will never come to our aid on the subject of emotions, because emotions are *individual* and science is only interested in the *general*. This represents a basic difference between the left hemisphere world of science and the right hemisphere. Even in the case of the study of human nature itself, science takes as significant only the general, the average (which represents no one in particular) and avoids the individual, which is in every case unique. The psychologist who studies aggressive behavior, for example, is interested only in those characteristics which create a syndrome of aggression, but can draw no useful conclusion from any one individual aggressive person. Art is just the reverse. We might say: The scientist dreads the presence of individuality as the death of science; the artist dreads the loss of individuality as the death of art.

> The reason why scientific description, so far from helping expression, actually damages it, is that description generalizes. To describe a thing is to call it a thing of such and such a kind; to bring it under a conception, to classify it. Expression on the contrary, individualizes ... Expressing an emotion has something to do with becoming conscious of it.[7]

7 R. Collingwood, *Principles of Art* (London: Oxford, 1938), 112.

The other arts, such as painting and sculpture, are also not nearly as effective as music in terms of the observer's self-discovery. The distinction with music in this regard is what makes music so different as to not really be part of 'the arts.' It is true that the painter can express *his* emotions on the canvas. But before the observer can hope to find some insight for himself he must first get past this extra step—engaging the eyes to look at the canvas before he can contemplate the artist's idea and then, eventually, seek insight for himself. Music, alone among the 'arts,' is a *direct* communication between composer and listener. And that is why music has such an immediate impact on every listener's feelings and why we speak of music being the international language—because the emotions are also genetically international.

And so we propose that Music Education must take on the responsibility of educating the emotional nature of the child, the half of the child's personality that the traditional curriculum, if not society itself, ignores. Music education needs to be in the school where a child becomes aware of, begins to explore and understand and finds a means of expressing his own personal emotional being. Music Education can do this, it is inseparable from the best of musical training and no one else in the school building is prepared to do it.

Music Education and the Child's Emotional Template

> Beethoven was the first man who used music with absolute integrity as the expression of his own emotional life ... In thus fearlessly expressing himself, he has, by his common humanity, expressed us as well, and shown us how beautifully, how strongly, how trustworthily we can build with our own selves.
> George Bernard Shaw

Music gives the listener the opportunity to explore their experiential right hemisphere, to discover their individual emotional identity and to contemplate their reaction to that discovery. The composer, Roger Sessions, maintained nothing else could do this as well.

> Emotion is specific, individual, and conscious; music goes deeper than this, to the energies which animate our psychic life, and out of these creates a pattern which has an existence, laws, and human significance of its own. It reproduces for us the most intimate essence the tempo and the energy, of our spiritual being; our tranquility and our restlessness, our animation and our discouragement, our vitality and our weakness—all, in fact, of the fine shades of dynamic variation of our inner life. It reproduces these far more directly and more specifically than is possible through any other medium of human communication.[8]

[8] *The Composer and his Message*, 1941.

This opportunity to explore one's experiential self is made possible due to the general and specific nature of emotion in music. Music does not communicate a specific form of emotion, but the 'quintessence' of that emotion. Wagner described this as follows:

> Music does not express the passion, love, or longing of such-and-such an individual on such-and-such an occasion, but passion, love or longing in itself.[9]

[9] Quoted in William Ashton Ellis, *Wagner's Prose Works* (New York: Broude), op. cit., VII, 81.

Listeners then take this generalized form in and simultaneously sift it through their own right hemisphere bank of experiences with that emotion. Therefore, with the listener the emotion takes on a specific form, or as Wagner then pointed out, it is in this way that Music allows us to 'gaze into the inmost Essence of ourselves.' This is the *only* way a listener can understand the emotions in music *as an individual*.

The key to this is not well symbolized by the word 'reflection,' which can mean meditation to no final effect. It is better if we use the word, 'reflexion,' which means the student hears the emotions in the music and it reflects back to him and causes him to become aware of *his* emotions. Then education can begin.

But, we may ask, will the listener perceive the same emotion as the composer? In the general form, yes, because of the genetic universality of emotions themselves. As long as it is authentic music, the listener cannot fail to perceive the generalized form of the emotion. Liszt summarizes these two aspects of musical communication as follows:

> Even though, in accordance with the propensity of his imagination, the individual clothes these passions and feelings with images of his own, he will be unable to deceive himself about the sort of temperamental activity which the composer intended his work to evoke.[10]

[10] Letter to August Kiel, September 8, 1855.

The contemporary researcher, Clynes, speculates on how our self-discovery/self-education process at this moment develops.

> We seem to be learning something, although not in the conventional sense of forming a new memory. Rather, we discover an aspect of what we already are but have neglected to cultivate. At first we may imagine particular situations in order to help us fantasize. Soon, though, we can experience and express an emotion without specific imagery. At a further stage, new imagery may spontaneously arise.
>
> ...
>
> It seems that when a person imagines and repeatedly expresses a single emotion—and then another emotion—and then another—and so on through an ordered range of primary emotions, the result is a feeling of satisfaction, well-being and deepened insight into one's own emotional life and the lives of others.[11]

[11] Manfred Clynes, 'The Pure Pulse of Musical Genius,' *Psychology Today*, July, 1974.

It is through this process, as Goethe explained, that we become better persons.

> When we encounter that which is great, beautiful, significant, it need not be remembered from the outside, need not be hunted up and laid hold of, as it were. Rather, from the beginning, it must be woven into

the fabric of our inmost self, must become one with it, create a new and better self in us and thus live and become a productive force in our lives.[12]

To this point listener and performer of music experience this emotion alike. But the performer now goes a significant step beyond the listener, as he now expresses his specific emotion in an immediate and direct, physical form. This externalizing process of expression allows the player to come to understand even more clearly his own emotional self. It follows, therefore, that learning how to play the clarinet is not the *important* thing; the important thing is that by learning to play the clarinet, the clarinet can serve as the vehicle for the student to discover music—and himself. One can also say there is nothing important about symphony orchestras; the important thing is the music they play and what that contributes to the listener.

The contribution that music makes is therefore not only one of balancing the American educational institution, but balancing the individual as well. The person who truly knows himself, is a person who will more likely have the courage to *be* himself, or as Mahler put it,

> The point is not to take the world's opinion as a guiding star, but to go one's way in life.[13]

Norman Cousins observed how important this sense of direction is when transposed to the level of society at large.

> One of the biggest needs of the school is not to teach people to do things, but to help them to understand what they are doing. Nothing is easier than to create a society of people in motion. Nothing is more difficult than to keep them from going nowhere.[14]

Self-discovery of one's emotional self through music is a value available to all students—if only music education were available to all students to guide them in this journey of discovery.

> Think what may happen to conceptual learning in music education if the day ever comes when we actually begin to demonstrate real concern for the individual needs of each student in our schools as those needs related to the expression of human feeling through music.[15]

[12] Quoted in *The New Yorker*, July 27, 1992, 65.

[13] Quoted in Alma Mahler, *Gustav Mahler* (New York: Viking Press, 1969), 216. This expression of confidence reminds me of another, by Martin Luther. He said, 'I have always loved music. Those who have mastered this art are of good stuff. They are fit for any task.'

[14] Norman Cousins, 'The Taxpayers's Revolt: Act Two,' *Saturday Review*, September 16, 1978, 56.

[15] James C. Carlsen, 'Concept Learning—Its Starts with a Concept of Music,' *Music Educators Journal*, November, 1973.

What happens when we continue to ignore this part of the student is expressed vividly by the famous newscaster, Paul Harvey:

> Our schools tend to refine intellects but neglect to discipline emotions.
> And undisciplined emotions keep getting us into trouble.
> The ugliest headlines are about somebody who may have been smart as all get-out—smart enough to be a bank executive or a politician or a scientist.
> But if emotionally colorblind, he's an unguided missile inevitably destined to self-destruct.
> Without the arts—including music—we risk graduating young people who are 'right-brain damaged.'
> For anyone to grow up complete, music education is imperative.[16]

[16] Paul Harvey, American Broadcasting Company, 1991.

The central focus if we are to concentrate on helping the student identify and develop his emotional template is the music[17] itself. Helping the student to identify his own emotional template through listening (even players need to be listeners) and then as educators helping to teach the goals of appropriate emotional development. To do this we will have to develop new materials for the music teachers at all levels, with the appropriate objectives and goals. It is an entirely new branch of music education and we must begin from the beginning.

[17] In music education the education, the curriculum, is the music. Anything else the teacher talks about may be important but it is not music. Harmony, for example, is not music; it is grammar.

At the same time we must also learn how to *describe* the element of feeling in music. But can left hemisphere language describe right hemisphere emotions? Well, we do this all the time in ordinary life, as when we say, 'I am mad!' Clearly we are aware of our own emotions. Recent research by UCLA psychologist Matthew Liberman and his colleagues suggests that just such labeling has a positive effect on negative emotions—something proponents of meditation have long argued.

> When the participants chose labels for the negative emotions, activity in the right ventrolateral prefrontal cortex region—an area associated with thinking in words about emotional experiences—became more active, whereas activity in the amygdale, a brain region involved in emotional processing, was calmed.[18]

[18] 'Brain Scans Reveal Why Meditation Works,' reported in Yahoo, LiveScience, June 30, 1007.

Of all the areas of our training as music educators, this has been the poorest. We are trained to talk about every kind of detail of notation and technique, but not feeling. Music Education has approached music as a technical discipline which can be taught and learned, but has left the most important part of music, its ability to communicate emotions and feelings, as an impenetrable mystery. One MENC publication, for example, stated that,

> through the processes of conceptual development children 'can grow' in their understanding of everything there is in music that makes it what it is except for the *mysterious* and *magical* processes by which it becomes more than the sum of its parts and through which it transcends the intellectual, or closed, system.[19]

[19] Charles L. Gary, ed., *The Study of Music in the Elementary School: A Conceptual Approach* (Washington, D. C.: MENC, 1967), 4.

Another music educator wrote that peak music experiences are more than the sum of their parts and that,

> by some *mysterious alchemy* they evoke in the listener such a response that he is never again the same.[20]

[20] Abraham Schwadron, 'Are We Ready for Aesthetic Education?,' *Music Educators Journal*, October, 1973.

I regard it as a dereliction of duty to write off the most important part of music, its content of feeling, as a 'mysterious alchemy.' I also regard this as the single most important role the music teacher has, to help the student learn to know his experiential self through music. To do this we must learn how to talk about what it is in music which contains and communicates feelings.

What one reads in the field of music can often be confusing. For example, the following statement by Stravinsky is sometimes taken to mean music has no emotional content.

> I consider that music is, by its very nature, powerless to express anything at all, whether a feeling, an attitude of mind, a psychological mood, a phenomenon of nature, etc. ... if, as is nearly always the case, music appears to express something, this is only an illusion, and not a reality.[21]

Igor Stravinsky

[21] Stravinsky, *Chronicle of My Life*, English translation, 91-92.

We are confident that what Stravinsky really meant was the music cannot represent something else. One can write a composition called the *Moldau*, but music cannot really be the Moldau.

Mendelssohn, on the other hand, while confessing very strong images in music seems to suggest he cannot attach words to them.

> People usually complain that music is so ambiguous; that it is so doubtful what they ought to think when they hear it; whereas everyone understands words. With me it is entirely the converse. And not only with regard to an entire speech, but also with individual words; these, too, seem to me to be so ambiguous, so vague, and so easily misunderstood in comparison with genuine music, which fills the soul with a thousand things better than words. The thoughts which are expressed to me by a piece of music which I love are not too indefinite to be put into words, but on the contrary too definite.[22]

[22] Letter to Marc Andre Souchay, October 5, 1842.

But everyone would surely recognize that music does convey specific emotional content, even if we are not sure how it works. May I offer the following experiment? Try singing the beginning of Handel's 'Hallelujah Chorus.' Now, sing it again, but replace the word 'Hallelujah' with the word, 'Crucifixus.' It doesn't work does it? But why doesn't it work? Is it only because we are *used* to the other word? No, the answer is that those particular notes and harmonies are the *wrong* ones for the specific emotional content of the word, 'Crucifixus.'

Clearly music communicates emotion. To consider this further, we must return for a moment to the consideration of language in general.

The earliest writing we know of early man are the pictures in the caves of France, dating from the last Ice Age. In a written language composed of pictures, as one also finds in the Egyptian tomb paintings, and in the ancient Asian languages, you have a language in which the written symbol is synonymous with one's experience (the symbol for 'cat' is a picture of a cat).

With regard to the development of left hemisphere language, a fundamental change occurred with the introduction of the much more efficient phonetic writing (now 'c-a-t' represents a cat, but does not look like a cat). This had the effect of putting a barrier between man's experience and his language, as explained by Marshall McLuhan:

> The phonetic alphabet did not change or extend man so drastically just because it enabled him to read. Tribal culture had already coexisted with other written languages for thousands of years. But the phonetic alphabet was radically different from the older and richer hieroglyphic or ideogrammic cultures. The writing of Egyptian, Babylonian, Mayan and Chinese cultures were an extension of the senses in that they gave pictorial expression to reality, and they demanded many signs

to cover the wide range of data in their societies—unlike phonetic writing which uses semantically meaningless letters to correspond to semantically meaningless sounds and is able, with only a handful of letters, to encompass all meanings and all languages. This achievement demanded the separation of both sights and sounds from their semantic and dramatic meanings in order to render visible the actual sound of speech, thus placing a barrier between men and objects and creating a dualism between sight and sound. It divorced the visual function from the interplay with the other senses and thus let to the rejection from the consciousness of vital areas of our sensory experience and to the resultant atrophy of the unconscious. the balance of the sensorium—or Gestalt interplay of all the senses—and the psychic and social harmony it engendered was disrupted, and the visual function was overdeveloped. This was true of no other writing system.[23]

[23] Marshall McLuhan, 'An Interview,' *Playboy*, March, 1969.

Once man turned to this new kind of writing, where the language-picture no longer corresponds with his experience, things in our rational world become confusing.

> Verbal identifications and confused abstractions begin at a tender age … language is no more than crudely acquired before children begin to suffer from it, and to misinterpret the world by reason of it.[24]

[24] Stuart Chase, *The Tyranny of Words* (New York: Harcourt, Brace, 1938), 56.

Another very important point is that from that moment we needed an intermediary, a teacher, to connect *us* with our language. Someone has to answer our questions, 'Why isn't *gnat* spelled with an *n*?' or 'When do we use *to*, *too*, or *two*?'

The development of our *right* hemisphere language, music, followed much the same course. Although early man had no pictorial equivalent for his music, his music *was* a means of directly communicating his feelings. This was such an effective system of communication that no further 'improvements' were needed over a great period of time.

The 'improvement' which came was music's equivalent of a phonetic alphabet, and we call it musical notation. In the case of instrumental music of Western Europe, this period was relatively recent, the late Middle Ages. As with left hemisphere language, once notation arrived it also required an intermediary, a Kapellmeister, teacher or conductor, to connect the musician's experience with the notation, to show him how you really play what is on paper. But as Wagner points out, even at that the written form of the music remains ambiguous.

Even today, although we have accustomed ourselves to a most minute notation of the nuances of phrasing, the more talented conductor often finds himself obliged to teach his musicians very weighty, but delicate shadings of expression by *viva voce* explanation; and these communications, as a rule, are better understood and heeded, than the written signs.[25]

[25] Ellis, op. cit., IV, 192.

In another place,[26] Wagner discusses the development of the dominance of the left hemisphere, and the separation of man from his feelings, in terms remarkably similar to McLuhan. 'Understanding,' by which he means what we call today the rational left hemisphere,

[26] ibid., II, 230ff.

> through the process of imagination acquired a language by which it would make itself intelligible *alone* and in a direct ratio: as the rational man became more intelligible the feeling man became less. In modern Prose we speak a language which we do not understand as being related to Feeling, since its connection with the objects, whose impression on our faculties first generated the roots of speech (pictures), has become lost to us.

It follows, he says, that once Understanding (the left hemisphere) developed a language according to the logic of that hemisphere,

> we must unconditionally obey when we want to impart our thoughts ... [and] to make ourselves thus far intelligible according to a given norm, in which we are to think and to subjugate our feelings in order that we may communicate to someone else's [left brain] an aim of our left brain. Our Feelings can only be inadequately *described* in this left brain language.

Since our feelings can not communicate in traditional language,

> it was altogether consequent that Feeling should have sought a refuge from absolute intellectual-speech by fleeing to absolute tone-speech, our Music of today.

This entire subject has been made very difficult by the men who invented our modern notational system for music. They were mathematicians, writing at the direction of the Church which wanted to discourage all kinds of emotions among early

Christians. Consequently, they invented a notational system which to this day has not one single symbol representing any emotion![27]

Nevertheless, in spite of the Church, music does express emotions and they are universally understood. Therefore, one should be able to identify a specific emotion in specific combinations of notes. Manfred Clynes, who had conducted extensive studies into the universal expression of emotions, has reached the same conclusion through his research.

> We can also look at the language of music from a scientific perspective; for it's a fact that music involves emotions, and it's possible to predict which emotions it will involve. A good composer who wants his music to communicate joy can do exactly that ... Music, in other words, is a form of communication that transmits emotion, and speaks about emotion in precise ways.[28]

For Wagner, the task of the composer is to craft this emotional thought into its most condensed and refined form, which he refers to in other places as the *Melos*. It is in this process that he finds the fundamental distinction between the composer and the writer of words.

> To address the Feeling to any degree, the Poet wandered into that vague diffuseness in which he became the delineator of a thousand details, intended to set a definite shape before the imagination as clearly as possible. But the imagination, bombarded by a host of motley details, only master the proffered object by trying to grasp these perplexing details one by one, thereby losing itself in the function of pure Understanding ... The composer's purpose, on the other hand, is to condense an endless element of Feeling into a definite point in order that it might be understood.[29]

My explanation for how emotions are contained in music is more natural, for I believe it lies with the natural overtone series which man has heard, on some level, with respect to every sound. Just as we know a single tone also generates a major key tonality, so I believe it follows that in man's use of these materials over thousands of years certain associations with emotions became, by common usage, an understood form of the communication of feelings through his music.

[27] When one recalls that music and musicians got along just fine for a million years or so without any notational system, one has to wonder if by inventing one we lost more than we gained.

[28] Manfred Clynes, 'The Pure Pulse of Musical Genius,' *Psychology Today*, July, 1974.

[29] ibid., II, 277ff.

Although it has become a cliché that music in a major key is 'happy,' and music in a minor key is 'sad,' I do not believe that the major–minor key system is the primary medium of emotional communication in music. This is because in a major key one finds important minor chords, and in a minor key one finds important major chords. For me, harmony is much more significant with regard to the movement of music through time, for example, than for emotions.

I believe what communicates emotions through music is the notes themselves, as they appear in intervals and melodic groupings. There has been some clinical research as well which suggests that melody is the primary vehicle for conveying emotion in music. There is a wonderful book by Deryck Cooke called *The Language of Music*[30] which demonstrates this brilliantly. He gives many musical examples, from several centuries, which work something like this. If you were to play on a piano, in the key of C minor, the melodic steps 1–2–3–4–5–6–5, surely we can agree that the Ab (6) produces a distinctly painful emotion. On the other hand, if you play the same scale steps in C major, the A (natural) now takes on the emotional quality of child-like innocence, as one finds, for example, in the 'Fourteen Angels guard our sleep,' in Humperdinck's *Hansel and Gretel*, or in the ancient tune, 'In dulci jubilo.'

[30] Clarendon Paperbacks, 1959.

The important thing for music education of the future is to guard against thinking of the emotions in music as a metaphor, even though we may use analogy in language to describe them. One finds this mistake in the following:

> The soul of every people is found in its songs, its images, its dances, its stories. Our best educators have always seen in them the energy that synthesizes true learning. The arts are the source of the metaphors that connect thought to experience. They illuminate the human prospect. They are basic to education because they are a universal language; to be illiterate here is to be blind, mute and deaf at the most fundamental level—that of the spirit.[31]

[31] *The Report of the National Commission of Music Education* (Reston: MENC, 1991), 1.

With regard to Music, this is simply wrong! Music is *not* a metaphor for anything; it is the *direct communication* of our feelings.

Nevertheless, some educators have refused to believe there is anything universal about music and emotions at all. Abraham Schwadron, for example, once wrote,

> Psychological studies have indicated that emotive responses to music are largely learned and culturally determined; that music is not a universal language; that feelings of 'sadness' caused by a minor mode is a learned response, not a natural, universal, magical, or God-given one; and that responses to new or different styles of music require relearning and a modification of listening habits.[32]

[32] Abraham Schwadron, 'Are We Ready for Aesthetic Education,' *Music Educators Journal*, October, 1973.

We know today that whatever 'Psychological studies' he read were misinformed. This viewpoint is incorrect throughout. Our emotive responses to music are *not* learned, they are biologically passed on to us through evolution. If we can say they are learned, we can only mean what we should be doing as music educators: helping children *learn to identify* their emotions through music.

I agree with Theodore Wood that it is through the *emotions* that we can reach our students, not through the conceptualized and abstracted elements of music—teach them though we must.

> It seems that it is literally impossible for one to speak directly about an art work. Neither can one, especially a latter-day aesthetician, afford to be purely subjective, because that becomes mere value judgment. But what about something in between? Why not choose an approach to aesthetic evaluation that somehow bridges the gap between work and perceiver? Might there not be an element that both work and perceiver have in common on which evaluation could be based?
>
> Neither the ancients nor the moderns have been unaware that 'emotion' is this kind of common element. Indeed, there seems little doubt in many minds that emotion dwells in both the work and the perceiver. Furthermore, the idea of emotion at least implies value and morality, two attributes aestheticians and philosophers are constitutionally loath to abandon.[33]

[33] Theodore Wood, 'What has Happened to the Arts?,' *Music Educators Journal*, October, 1973.

I believe the emotional content of music is real. I believe what attracts us to the great performer of music is largely his unusual ability to define and communicate this emotional content of the music for us. Manfred Clynes, who had conducted extensive research on the patterns of emotional expression, which he calls 'essentic forms,' describes it this way:

> Thus music is truly a language of essentic forms. Musicians use this language in order to communicate emotions and qualities to others who recognize the language. Access to essentic forms is part of what

musical talent means: the most gifted musicians are those who are able to achieve the greatest purity of essentic form. The purest forms are the most recognizable by others; they communicate with the greatest power to transform. Clearly, there is nothing arbitrary about this talent. Talent does not amount merely to 'somebody's opinion.' Talent is real.[34]

34 Clynes, op. cit.

I also believe that it is the emotional content that the great artist himself looks for in music, and not the abstracted, data elements, the grammar really, of music we were all taught, under the name 'music education,' in school. In this regard, I was struck when reading, in an unpublished, private diary, some notes Wagner made in 1864, when he first encountered the C-Sharp Minor Quartet, op. 131, of Beethoven. In these notes for himself, he did not write of the beginning key and where it modulated to, nor of the elements of melody, harmony, or rhythm, nor of counterpoint, scoring, articulations or dynamics.

This is what he wrote:

> (Adagio) Melancholy morning-prayer of a deeply suffering heart: (Allegro) graceful apparition, rousing fresh desire of life. (Andante and variations). Charm, sweetness, longing, love. (Scherzo) Whim, humor, high spirits. (Finale) Passing over to resignation. Most sorrowful renunciation.[35]

35 Ellis, op. cit., VIII, 386.

And which is more expressive of the music, his language or if he had instead written in the usual fashion of music theory of only the grammar—key, modulations, harmony, rhythm, etc.? I recall once as a graduate student being forced to take pencil to score and make a chordal analysis, placing Roman numerals and figured-bass numbers, under every single chord of every beat in the entire Third Symphony of Beethoven. It took some weeks to do this, on top of my full-time duties in the military, but I can recall vividly my first thought when I finished and laid down my pencil. The thought immediately occurred to me that I had learned nothing. Oh, to be sure I could have written a lengthy academic paper on, let us say, 'The Use of the Subdominant Chord in Beethoven's Third Symphony.' But I learned nothing about the music.

The fundamental paradox which must be faced by music education is this: The fundamental nature of music is to communicate emotion, but we do not teach the fundamental nature of the subject of music. We only teach on the periphery of music and no other school subject does this. If you teach math you teach fundamentals, not things on the periphery. Therefore I believe that our first purpose as music educators must be to teach the fundamental nature and purpose of music. Our first goal should be to help the student come to know himself on an emotional level, to help him learn to communicate on that level through music and to help him become a balanced and stable adult. No other school subject can do this.

I hope the reader can see the magnificent opportunity this is. We may not only improve our teaching of music but also make an important, even historic, contribution to education—the first education-wide attempt to help the student learn to know himself on the emotional side of his being. If you only stop to reflect on how society has so completely failed the youth in this regard, sending them out into the streets to discover their emotional identity for themselves, one can imagine how great would be the contribution of music education to the nation.

The second paramount new purpose for music education which is needed for the future is closely related.

The Second Paramount New Purpose: Music Education Must Return to Taking Responsibility for Moral Values

LITERATURE FROM THE MOST ANCIENT TIMES frequently refers to the use of music in education for the purpose of forming character and shaping behavior. This was widely believed and practiced in every succeeding century of the modern age and in the United States until the 1960s. When I was a student at the University of Michigan in the 1950s I heard William D. Revelli once declare, 'The boy who blows a horn will never blow a safe.' Perhaps so, for consider the results of a prison survey in 1964:

> In 80% of the prisons in all states of the Union who responded to questionnaires, there were no men or women who had had any form of music education before they committed the crimes for which they were incarcerated.[36]

[36] Reported in *The Journal of Music Therapy*, March, 1964, 13.

The ancient tradition of using only aesthetic music in the academic world began to rapidly change in the United States in the 1960s with the introduction of indoor entertainment music. The dance band appeared in schools, quickly renaming itself 'jazz band' or 'big band.' I recall during the 1970s when walking through a university rehearsal hall and seeing on the floor a tenor saxophone part to a 'chart' called *Sock it to me, baby!* I could not help but reflect on how far our philosophy of music education had departed from Plato. Next came 'world music,' under which title the most trivial music was allowed as necessary to education. One music education specialist went so far as to propose his theory that our musical literature in school should be like a buffet table—put everything out there and let the student select what he wants to. This embarrassing dereliction of educational ethics is like in astronomy classes handing out to the students the theories of everyone from Ptolemy, who thought the earth was the center of the entire universe, to Kepler, who thought the placement of stars was based on common figures of geometry, and then telling the student to just believe whatever theories about astronomy they like.

Meanwhile, while thus leaving our students to wander the halls of academia in ethical confusion, outside the classroom our students are surrounded with the music of the 'Three R's,' rock, reggae and rap. If you older teachers have ever wondered what you are hearing when you hear rap, here is a translation by an Oakland High School student of a song from the album *Ready to Die*, by the Notorious B.I.G. This is what our students are listening to, and they, unlike you, understand it.

Lyrics:
First things first, I poppa, freaks all the honeys
Dummies—playboy bunnies, those wantin' money
Those the ones I like 'cause they don't get nathan'
But penetration, unless it smells like sanitation
Garbage, I turn like doorknobs
Heart throb, never, black and ugly as ever
However, I stay coochied down to the socks
Rings and watch filled with rocks

Translation:
As a general rule, I perform deviant sexual acts with women of all kinds, including but not limited to those with limited intellect, nude magazine models, and prostitutes. I particularly enjoy sexual encoun-

ters with the latter group as they are generally disappointed in the fact that they only receive penile intercourse and nothing more, unless of course, they douche on a consistent basis. Although I am extremely unattractive, I am able to engage in these types of sexual acts with some regularity. Perhaps my sexuality is somehow related to my fancy and expensive jewelry.[37]

That's where we are. Maybe now in thinking of music education of the future it is an appropriate time to step back and reconsider the reintroduction of something believed for thousands of years but which has totally fallen from discussion in American music education. The subject is the moral values which derive from music.

History is rich with great minds who argued that this was a basic characteristic of music itself. What Confucius (551–479 BC) once observed might as well describe our society as his!

> If you would know if a people be well governed, if its laws be good or bad, examine the music it practices.[38]

In the West, philosophers from a very early period noticed the great impact which music had on its listeners. They attributed this to a special quality of hearing, one of the five senses. In the case of all the other senses the immediate impression seems outside the body. In vision we concentrate on something we see outside the body; we are here and we see a great waterfall over there. The same with touch; the chief impression is the feeling as we touch something outside the body. Music, however, you cannot see, even while its impact is often clearly visible on the face of the listener. From these observations the older philosophers concluded that of the senses, only the ear offered a route inside the body. This was the explanation, they believed for the power of music over morals and manners.

Boethius (475–524 AD), a famous mathematician, observed, for example:

> There happen to be four mathematical disciplines [arithmetic, music, geometry, and astronomy], the other three share with music the task of searching for truth; but music is associated not only with speculation but with morality as well.[39]

[37] http://www.bizbag.com/Misc%20articles/Rap%20Lyrics%20Translated.htm

[38] Quoted in Shapiro, op. cit., 233.

[39] Boethius, *Fundamentals of Music*, trans., Calvin Bower (New Haven: Yale University Press), I, i.

The first great philosopher of the English Baroque was Francis Bacon (1561–1626). In his *Natural History* he devotes a lengthy discussion to the role of music in affecting manners and attempts to explain how it works.

Francis Bacon

> It has been anciently held and observed, that the sense of hearing and the kinds of music most in operation upon manners; as to encourage men and make them warlike; to make them soft and effeminate; to make them grave; to make them light; to make them gentle and inclined to pity; etc. The cause is, for that the sense of hearing strikes the spirits more immediately than the other senses, and more incorporeally than the smelling. For the sight, taste, and feeling, have their organs not of so present and immediate access to the spirits, as the hearing has. And as for the smelling (which indeed works also immediately upon the spirits, and is forcible while the object remains), it is with a communication of the breath or vapor of the object odorate; but harmony, entering easily, and mingling not at all, and coming with a manifest motion, doth by custom of often affecting the spirits and putting them into one kind of posture, alter not a little the nature of the spirits, even when the object is removed.[40]

[40] *Natural History*, Section 114, in James Spedding, ed., *The Works of Francis Bacon* (Cambridge: Cambridge University Press, 1869).

This relationship which music was believed to have on the shaping of character and on shaping manners is testified to throughout Western history.[41]

According to Strabo, the government of ancient Egypt placed musicians in charge of the development of character in the young.[42] Plutarch (46–119 AD) gave a bit more detail, recalling that the Greeks 'were so careful to teach their children music,'

[41] See the earlier essays in this series, Nrs. 20, 38 and 39 for much more material.

[42] Quoted in Lise Manniche, *Music and Musicians in Ancient Egypt* (London: British Museum Press, 1991), 41.

> for they deemed it requisite by the assistance of music to form and compose the minds of youth to what was decent, sober, and virtuous; believing the use of music beneficially efficacious to incite to all serious actions.[43]

[43] 'Concerning Music.'

And in one place, Plato seems to have made this purpose a part of the very definition of music.

> And the sound of the voice which reaches and educates the soul, we have ventured to term music.[44]

[44] *Laws*, 672e.

The early Christians emphasized the power of music to affect manners, as we see already in the second century in the writings of Clement of Alexandria.

> Music is then to be handled for the sake of the embellishment and composure of manners.[45]

[45] Clement of Alexandria, 'The Miscellanies,' Book VI, xi.

By late Middle Ages fantastic stories of the power of music to change manners appear, such as Guido's claim[46] that music saved a young lady in stopping a rapist by changing his intent and Cotton's belief that music can disarm bandits.[47]

During the Renaissance, we find the sixteenth-century Italian philosopher, Giulio del Bene, recommending 'Through music learn to be well ordered and constituted in our minds.'[48] In fact, Vincenzo Galilei (1533–1591) believed it was impossible to find a man who is truly a musician who is also of a vicious character.[49]

Among the French humanists known as the Pléiade was an important philosopher, Pontus de Tyard. In his *Solitaire premier, ou, Prose des Muses & de la fureur Poetique* (1552), he contended that the purpose of music, in particular, was to raise the soul from the lowest point from which it has fallen.[50] Similar references to the power of music to affect the soul can be found in Calvin and Luther, the latter observing,

> Music is a semi-discipline and taskmistress, which makes people milder and more gentle, more civil and more sensible.[51]

[46] See *Hucbald, Guido, and John on Music*, trans., Warren Babb (New Haven: Yale University Press, 1978), 160.

[47] ibid., 114ff.

[48] Quoted in Claude V. Palisca, *Humanism in Italian Renaissance Musical Thought* (New Haven: Yale University Press, 1985), 337.

[49] Galilei, 'Dialogo della musica antica e della moderna.'

[50] Quoted in Frances Yates, *The French Academies of the Sixteenth Century* (London: University of London, 1947; Nendeln: Kraus Reprint, 1968), 80ff.

[51] Quoted in Walter Buszin, 'Luther on Music,' in *The Musical Quarterly* (January, 1946), 92.

Similarly, Nicholaus Listenius (ca. 1500–1550), who studied at Wittenberg in 1529, when both Luther and Melanchthon were teaching there, wrote in his treatise, *Musica* (1537),

> Music influences souls to humanity, suavity, even-temper; it restrains all immoderate affections, grief, wrath; it represses violence and obscene desires … This art invites the soul to virtue.[52]

[52] Nicolaus Listenius, *Musica*, trans., Albert Seay (Colorado Springs: Colorado College Music Press, 1975), 1.

We also find some interesting comments on our subject in sixteenth-century German music treatises. Andreas Ornithoparchus, author of *Musice active micrologus* of 1517, was associated with several universities, in particular Leipzig and Tubingen. The very purpose of his book, he announces, is to provide the youth of all of Germany with a book which would introduce them to good fashions, the honest delights of music and 'little by little stir them to virtuous actions.' In this, he continues,

> Among those things by which the mind of man is wont to be delighted, I can find nothing that is more great, that appeals to any age or sex ... There is no breast so savage and cruel, which is not moved with the touch of this delight. For it drives away cares, persuades men to gentleness, represses anger, nourishes arts, promotes concord, inflames heroic minds to gallant deeds, cures vice, breeds virtues and nourishes them ... Therefore this Art is of a holy, sweet, heavenly, divine, fair and blessed nature.[53]

53 Ornithoparchus, *Musicae active mirologus* and Dowland, *Introduction: Containing the Art of Singing* (New York: Dover, 1973), 117ff.

And then there is that memorable comment by Handel, made in a letter to Lord Kinnoull, after the first London performance of the *Messiah*, on 23 March 1743:

> I should be sorry, my lord, if I have only succeeded in entertaining them; I wished to make them better.

This influence of music on man is also mentioned by the great composers of the nineteenth century. Let us only mention Wagner, who wrote precisely of the professional negligence of which we are guilty today.

> Music is able to work on taste, but also on *manners*: the first point will be disputed by no one, even in our day; but a direct relation to morality has not as yet been generally ascribed to Music, in fact it has even been judged as morally quite harmless. That is not so.[54]

54 'A National Theater,' in *Prose Works of Wagner*, op. cit., VII, 355.

It is only because we have forgotten Wagner's warning that this subject of the relationship of music and character development and manners has fallen from discussion in American music education. It was taken for granted until the 1960s but then became irrelevant as American music educators rushed to introduce new entertainment media into the schools.

But in their rush to swing the pendulum from the aesthetic to entertainment, music teachers lost sight of the most fundamental basis of music education. They forgot that in music education, the *music* is the education. This basic premise of music education has been clearly understood and commented on over many epochs. Many earlier philosophers were careful to specify that only 'good' music, or 'specially selected' music can accomplish the higher goals of music education. Here are a few examples.

Plato apparently took it for granted that the difference between good and 'vulgar' music was obvious and to him it was clear how this distinction affected the child's music preferences later on.

> And if a man be brought up from childhood to the age of discretion and maturity in the use of the orderly and severe music, when he hears the opposite he detests it, and calls it illiberal; but if trained in the sweet and vulgar music, he deems the severer kind cold and displeasing. So that while he who hears them gains no more pleasure from the one than from the other, the one has the advantage of making those who are trained in it better men, whereas the other makes them worse.[55]

[55] *Laws.*, 802.

In *The Clouds*, by Aristophanes (450–366 BC), we get a glimpse of the music education of boys destined to be professional lyre players. The quality of the music used for instruction was already an important issue, for we read,

> their lyres were strung
> Not to ignoble melodies, for they were taught
> A loftier key.[56]

[56] *Clouds*, 961ff.

The same emphasis on quality music also seems evident in Polybius (200–118 BC), in his history of Arcadia, when he writes 'For the practice of music, I mean *real* music, is beneficial to all men.'[57]

With the arrival of the Christian Era we find a comment by one of the early church fathers, Clement of Alexandria (ca. 150–215 AD), specifically speaking of the use of music to improve manners and he emphasizes the importance of using only *good* music for this purpose. What Clement calls 'superfluous music' is popular music, which has, of course, been around as long as music itself. The point is that popular music was not used in education until our time.

[57] Polybius, *The Histories*, IV.20.5ff, trans., W. R. Paton (Cambridge: Harvard University Press, 1954).

> Music is then to be handled for the sake of the embellishment and composure of manners. For instance, at a banquet we pledge each other while the music is playing; soothing by song the eagerness of

our desires, and glorifying God for the copious gift of human enjoyments, for His perpetual supply of the food necessary for the growth of the body and of the soul. But we must reject superfluous music, which enervates men's souls, and leads to variety,—now mournful, and then licentious and voluptuous, and then frenzied and frantic.[58]

[58] Clement of Alexandria, in 'The Miscellanies,' trans., William Wilson (Edinburgh: T. & T. Clark, 1884), Book VI, xi.

When Johannes de Grocheo, began his music treatise, *De Musica* (ca. 1300), with the caution that music in education must be used 'in the proper way,' he was referring to the choice of the music.

An understanding of music is necessary to those who wish to have a complete understanding of bodies moving and moved ... It is also good in a practical sense, for it corrects and improves the customs of men if used in the proper way.[59]

[59] Johannes de Garlandia, *De Mensurabili Musica*, trans., Stanley Birnbaum (Colorado Springs: Colorado Collge Music Press, 1978), 1.

Desideratum Erasmus (1469–1536), the greatest humanist, scholar and writer of prose of the early sixteenth century in the Low Countries, wrote at length on the dangers to the morals of young women of the vulgar popular music of his time.

Desideratum Erasmus

It is customary now among some nations to compose every year new songs which young girls study assiduously. The subject matter of the songs is usually the following: a husband deceived by his wife, or a daughter guarded in vain by her parents, or a clandestine affair of lovers. These things are presented as if they were wholesome deeds, and a successful act of profligacy is applauded. Added to pernicious subject matter are such obscene innuendoes, expressed in metaphors and allegories, that no manner of depravity could be depicted more vilely.

Many earn a livelihood in this occupation, especially among the Flemish. If laws were enforced, composers of such common ditties would be flogged for singing these doleful songs to the licentious. Men who publicly corrupt youth are making a living from crime, yet parents are found who think it a mark of good breeding if their daughters know such songs.

Antiquity considered music to belong to the liberal disciplines. Since musical sounds have great power to affect the soul of man...the ancients carefully distinguished musical modes, preferring the Dorian to others. They believed this matter to be so important that laws were enacted so that music would not be permitted in the state if it corrupted the minds of citizens.

But in our music, apart from obscenity in texts and subjects, how much is frivolity, how much is folly? There existed in former times a kind of performance in which, without words and only by pantomime, anything that was desired could be represented. In the same way in modern songs, even if the text is not sung, the foulness of the subject can be understood from the nature of the music. Then add to this the sound of frenetic pipes and noisy drums combining with a frenzy of movements. To such music young girls dance, to this they are accustomed, and yet we think there is no danger to their morals.[60]

The important English Church philosopher, Richard Hooker (1553–1600), a rational voice which attempted to counter the radical Puritans, shared the concern of Erasmus for the influence of vulgar music.

> In [music] the very image and character even of virtue and vice is perceived, the mind delighted with their resemblances, and brought by having them often iterated into a love of the things themselves. For which cause there is nothing more contagious and pestilent than some kinds of [music]; then some nothing more strong and potent unto good. And that there is such a difference of one kind from another we need no proof but our own experience.[61]

Juan Vives, author of a famous sixteenth-century book, *On Education*, contends that music should be part of education for the purpose of stabilizing the students' manners, but he is yet another who specifies the importance of using only good music.

> Only let the pupil practice pure and good music which, after the Pythagorean mode, soothes, recreates, and restores to itself the wearied mind of the student; then let it lead back to tranquility and tractability all the wild and fierce parts of the student's nature.[62]

In more recent times we find Wagner making this same point with respect to the quality of education.

> The acceptance of the empty for the sound is stunting everything we possess in the way of schools, tuition, academies and so on, by ruining the most natural feelings and misguiding the faculties of the rising generation.[63]

In terms of music education, his answer was clear.

> The true aesthetics and the sole intelligible history of music we must teach in no other way but by beautiful and correct performances of works of classical music.[64]

Richard Hooker

[60] Erasmus, *Opera omnia*, ed., J. Clericus (Leiden, 1703-1706), V, 717F, quoted in Clement A. Miller, 'Erasmus on Music,' in *The Musical Quarterly* [July, 1966], 347ff.

[61] Richard Hooker, *On the Laws of Ecclesiastical Polity*, V, xxxviii, in *The Works of Mr. Richard Hooker* (Oxford: Clarendon Press, 1888), II, 159.

Juan Vives

[62] ibid.

[63] 'On Poetry and Composition,' *Wagner's Prose Works*, op. cit., VI, 147.

[64] 'A Music School for Munich,' ibid., IV, 200.

An appropriate analogy by Schumann makes the same point.

> No children can be brought to healthy manhood on candy and pastry. Spiritual like bodily nourishment must be solid. The masters have provided it; cleave to them.

George Bernard Shaw could not understand why we should *want* to expose our children to anything but beautiful music.

> The notion that you can educate a child musically by any other means whatsoever except that of having beautiful music finely performed within its hearing, is a notion which I feel [forced] to denounce.[65]

[65] *Music in London, 1890–1894.*

These distinguished thinkers all point to the same basic fact which has been ignored by American music education for the past fifty years: the quality of music education cannot be separated from the quality of the music itself because the curriculum *is* the music.

These many testimonials to restricting music education to 'good' music are not simply reflections of personal choice in what is good music. Their conclusions are based on something much more basic which was first introduced by Aristotle under the term, *catharsis*. Generally it works like this: Aesthetic music (the modern term for 'good' music) reaches inside the listener and can even change the listener's life to some degree, while Entertainment music only seems to 'bounce off' the listener. Entertainment music can be interesting, fun and fully engrossing, but when it is over, it is over and soon forgotten. For these reasons, popular music can never be 'important.'

Aristotle coined the term 'catharsis' to describe the valuable purpose he found in Tragedy.

> Tragedy, then, is an imitation of an action that is serious, complete, and of a certain magnitude; in language embellished with each kind of artistic ornament, the several kinds being found in separate parts of the play; in the form of action, not of narrative; through pity and fear effecting the proper catharsis [*katharein*] of these emotions. By 'language embellished,' I mean language into which rhythm, harmony[66] and song enter. By 'the several kinds in separate parts,' I mean, that some parts are rendered through the medium of verse alone, others again with the aid of song.[67]

[66] The ancient Greeks used the word translated as 'harmony' to mean music.

[67] 'Poetics,' 1449b.24. The work is incomplete and the sections which discussed the use of music in tragedy, in particular, are lost. Later speculation on what the role of music *really* was in Greek Tragedy led to the creation of opera.

The Greek word, *katharein*, is rendered in dictionaries of our time as something like 'the purification or purgation of the emotions.'[68] This definition is based on a description of a sixteenth-century physician, Girolamo Cardano (1501–1576), who gives the phrase, 'cleansing of the spirit,' as a synonym of 'purge' in his definition of the parts of music.

> [Music's] usefulness is divided into three parts, for it pertains to instruction and study, or to the cleansing of the spirit, or to spending time pleasurably in leisure, tranquility, and freedom from the pressure of more serious matters. It is often said that emotions in music reflect weakened and enervated morals, but I believe such emotions consist of gentle virtues, and correspond to those more appropriate to action and also to those most divine virtues suitable for intellectual endeavor. Accordingly music celebrates those moral virtues which are especially appropriate to that useful quality which pertains to learning.[69]

We think a more familiar contemporary illustration of what Aristotle meant by this word can be found in our common experience in the cinema. One can think of going to the cinema with friends and during the film we are totally involved, we laugh, we cry. But as soon as the film ends, on the way out of the theater we immediately begin talking with our friends about other things, school, boy/girl friends and jobs, etc. On another occasion we go with friends to the cinema and when the film ends no one says a word, sometimes for a long time. We wish we could just sit there and that they would not turn on the lights. In the first example we were entertained. We were totally involved, but unaffected. In the second example the film reached us on a *deeper* level. It did not just 'bounce off.'[70] This is catharsis.

This term is frequently used in the field of drama criticism in the centuries following Aristotle, but also the idea of catharsis continued to be used by some philosophers in the field of music. The most important Renaissance writer to write of catharsis was the great theorist, Johannes Tinctoris (1435–1511). In writing of the composers he most respected (Dufay, Dunstable and Okeghem, etc.) he describes himself after hearing their music as being 'more refreshed and wiser.'[71] This new phrase, 'to be refreshed,' is one that will be used frequently to describe catharsis during the German Baroque.

---

[68] My *Webster's Ninth New Collegiate Dictionary*.

[69] Quoted in Clement Miller, *Hieronymus Cardanus, Writings on Music* (American Institute of Musicology, 1973), 105.

[70] The reader will easily recall similar examples of both experiences following concerts.

[71] *The Art of Counterpoint*, trans., Albert Seay (American Institute of Musicology, 1961), 14ff.

There is another Renaissance reference to catharsis which we really like. It is found in the music treatise, *Musica* (1537), by the German theorist Nicholaus Listenius, who was a student at Wittenberg when Luther was there. In this work he first defines music in the two familiar academic categories, the theoretical and practical (performance). Even in his definition of the performing musician, he seems to find for the listener an end beyond just listening to the music. The listener, he says, should be left with 'something more,' than the performance itself.

> Practical, whose goal is doing, is that which delights not only in the intricacies of skill, but extends into performance itself, leaving out no part of the act of performance. Hence the practical musician, who teaches others something more than the recognition of art, trains himself in it for the goal of any performance.

He employs this phrase again in a passage where he makes a real contribution to aesthetics by adding a third part to the traditional definition of music. In addition to the theoretical and the practical, he now adds what he calls the 'poetic.' By this he is thinking of the meaning left with the listener when the performance is concluded. This he calls '*total* performance.' It is most important and enlightening that he also observed in passing that the practical and the poetic always include the theoretical, 'but the reverse is not true.' When he says here that the total performance 'leaves something more' after the conclusion of the performance, he is speaking of catharsis exactly in the sense of our cinema analogy above.

> Poetic is that which is not content with just the understanding of the thing nor with only its practice, but which leaves something more after the labor of performance, as when music or a song of musicians is composed by someone whose goal is total performance and accomplishment. It consists of making or putting together more in this work which afterwards leaves the work perfect and absolute, which otherwise is artificially like the dead.

In previous chapters we have documented the fact that the Baroque musician was obsessed with finding ways to communicate emotion through music. The composers shared this new emphasis on emotions with the other musicians as is illustrated in Johann Scheibe's poem of 1739, 'Music which does not penetrate the heart or soul ... is quite dead.'[72] Composers now began to add forewords and dedications to their scores which clearly gave catharsis as the goal of their music. Thus we find in the score of Bach's *Clavier Ubung*, part III, and also in the 'Goldberg Variations,' a statement to the effect that his purpose was to 'refresh the spirits' of the listener. Similarly, when Bach was looking into a position in Halle, he was sent a contract which specified that the church music should have the result that 'the members of the Congregation shall be the more inspired and refreshed in worship.'[73]

We can document this transformation in the foreword of Georg Muffat's *Auserlesene Instrumental-Music* (1701). First, he explains that in his previous collections he has sought to draw 'liveliness and grace' from the 'Lullian well.' In other words, previously he wrote in the French style, whose goal contemporaries often referred to as 'tickling the ears.' Now, in the present collection Muffat says his goal is to present 'certain profound and unusual affects of the Italian manner.' The purpose of this music, as he makes very clear, is what we would call aesthetic music in the modern sense. That is, serious music intended for the contemplative listener. Muffat expresses it this way:

> These concerti, suited neither to the church ... nor for dancing ... [are] composed only for the express refreshment of the ear.

These early references speak of an experience which does not just 'bounce off' the listener. They are describing aesthetic music, not entertainment music. The quality of the literature is the key for music education, as we have stated before, music *is* the education, it *is* the curriculum.

Wagner once addressed this topic, under the title, 'Ethical relation of Music to the State.'[74]

> No less than Drama, Music is able to work on taste, yes, also on *manners*: the first point will be disputed by no one, even in our day; but a direct relation to morality has not as yet been generally ascribed to Music, in fact it has even been judged as morally quite harmless.
> This is not so. Could an effeminate and frivolous taste remain without influence on a man's morality? Both go hand in hand, and act reciprocally upon each other: not to refer to the Spartans, who for-

[72] Poem in honor of the publication of Johann Mattheson, *Der vollkommene Capellmeister* (1739), trans., Ernest Harriss (Ann Arbor: UMI Research Press, 1981), 74.

[73] Quoted in Hans T. David and Arthur Mendel, *The Bach Reader* (New York: Norton, 1966), 65.

[74] Quoted in William Ashton Ellis, ed., *Wagner's Prose Works* (New York: Broude), VII, 355ff.

bade a certain type of music as injurious to morals,—let us think back to our own immediate past; with tolerable certainty we may contend that those inspired by *Beethoven's* music have been more active and energetic citizens of the State than those bewitched by Rossini, Bellini and Donizetti, a class consisting for the most part of rich and lordly do-nothings. A speaking proof is further afforded by Paris: anyone might have observed during the last decades that in exact degree as the morals of Parisian society have rushed into that unexampled corruption, its music has foundered in a sphere of frivolous taste; one has only to hear the latest compositions of an Auber, Adam and so on, and to compare them with the odious dances performed in Paris at the time of Carnival, to perceive a terrible connection. If this rather proves that Morals operate on Music, yet the mutual relation of the two is manifest; it consequently is the State's affair to apply to this art, as well, that demand addressed by Kaiser Joseph to the Theater: 'that it shall work for the ennobling of taste *and* manners.'

Today we can speak from the perspective of considerably more evidence that it does indeed make a difference what music we expose our students to. On the experiential side we each are the product of different experiences, we arrive at music as listeners from different experiences, and the composer composes from different experiences. Therefore, experiences to which we give commonly accepted names have uncommon definitions. For example, we have the word 'love' in the English language, but what each person understands by that word is the sum of his own personal experiences. And, as everyone knows, not every 'love' experience is of the same quality, significance, nor has the same impact on one's life.

It is the same with music. With music notation a composer can, according to his purpose and ability, write music which communicates very superficial experiences or very profound experiences. I think the more profound the experience the composer wishes to communicate, the more inadequate the language is to express it. Therefore in the great masterpieces of Western European music, the notational language is only an incomplete shorthand offering clues to profound experiential truths which are incapable of notation in any symbolic language. This is what Mahler meant when he remarked that, 'the important things in Music are not found in the notes.' I think the art of teaching music is the art of teaching the student to experience what Mahler is talking about.

Because it is the experiential aspect of music which communicates to the listener (and I include here the player) we come to the real heart of the problem in music education. You can not separate the quality of the experience (the music) and the quality of the education. The music we give our students *becomes part of the experiential make-up of that student*. The experience shapes the person and it can not be avoided. If we want our students to have the best possible musical experience we must give them the best possible music. As Zoltan Kodaly stated it:

> Children should be taught with only the most musically valuable material. For the young, only the best is good enough. They should be led to masterpieces by means of masterpieces.

Thus will the music itself define the perimeters of the educational experience available to the student. If you set in front of the student a composition which is insignificant, then even the greatest teaching or the greatest performance will not raise the educational opportunity for the student above the level of insignificance. The reason for this was expressed by Bruno Walter. He pointed out that while a poor performance (or poor teaching) could diminish a great composition, the reverse does not hold true. You can not say that a great performance (or great teaching) will improve a composition, because a great performance will only bring into sharper focus those characteristics which make a poor composition poor.

This does not mean that in the selection of the music the role of the teacher ends. But it does mean that in the selection of the literature the teacher is clearly drawing the perimeter in which he and the student can work.

James C. Carlsen makes the point that experiential learning occurs in spite of ourselves:

> In the affective domain, the things we encounter in our everyday life do something to us. This happens constantly. We can't avoid it. Any event, any object, or any circumstance in which a person finds himself has the potential to affect his attitude or his emotional state. In spite of the attention being given these days to the inclusion of affective objectives in instruction, I think it's important that we understand that a person does not *learn* to be affected; he *is* affected in spite of what he might do. New experiences, or perhaps repeated experiences, can result in the discovery that new feelings or attitudes are developing,

but this does not happen because we *will* this affective change. On the contrary, it happens in spite of what we might have intended. Perhaps all that can be accomplished to expedite the development of a given affective response is to get the person to become receptive and to be in a permissive frame of being—one in which he will not fight off a particular change in his attitude or feeling toward a series of events.

But neither the motor activities of an individual nor his attitudes, feelings, or emotions can be construed essentially as conceptual operations. Although in our analysis of movements or feelings, we undoubtedly conceptualize them, the movements themselves and the feelings are not concepts.[75]

There is even extraordinary clinical evidence to suggest that something similar to 'You are What you Eat' happens with respect to our brain's response to our experiences. Experiences actually change the brain physically! Thus the choice the teacher makes with respect to the quality of music he sets before the child is a very serious responsibility, for it *literally* shapes the child.

The brain's neurons change the communication pathways among themselves in response to experience, says Dartmouth's Bharucha. Working with a computer model of brain cells called a neural network, Bharucha found that as he exposed the model to music, the layer of brain cells responsible for processing individual notes sent signals to another layer whose cells gradually became specialized for recognizing specific groups of notes, or chords. These cells in turn signaled a third layer of cells that gradually became responsible for recognizing groups of chords as belonging to particular keys. This hierarchical grouping occurred even though Bharucha gave the brain model no explicit instructions as to how the cells should connect themselves. Instead, the network simply organized itself in a manner that reflected the intrinsic organization of music itself.[76]

Now comes the bad news for music educators: *there is no middle ground*. Music literature must be judged as aesthetic or entertainment. A concert, for example, cannot be both. Even if only one entertainment work is given in an otherwise concert of aesthetic music, the listener will leave the hall believing he had an entertainment experience.

It follows that the music educator must think of himself as either an artist or an entertainer—he cannot have it both ways. The principle has been stated over and over since the time of

[75] James C. Carlsen, 'Concept Learning—It Starts with a Concept of Music,' *Music Educators Journal*, November, 1973.

[76] 'The Musical Brain,' *U. S. News & World Report*, June 11, 1990. Diana Deutsch, of the University of California, San Diego, has found some evidence to suggest that we hear the octave as such a pure interval due to the channeling of nerve impulses to the same nerve cell in the brain. See, 'What Happens When Music Meets the Brain,' *Wall Street Journal*, August 30, 1985.

Aristotle and artists who have not believed this and tried to be both anyway have always failed. Schumann once wrote of Viennese composers as an example of this failure.

> The same thing has been said, with the same result, of a hundred other Viennese composers; they want one thing, yet cannot give up the other; they must be artists, and yet please the crowd; boundless failures in this endeavor have not yet opened their eyes to the fact that nothing can be attained on such a path.[77]

77 Robert Schumann, 'Trios for Pianoforte, Violin, and Violoncello,' in *Neue Zeitschrift fur Musik*, 1842.

The problem in music education today is that it is so easy to respond to popularity, to please the crowd (not to mention parents and administrators) and in the process to turn an aesthetic educational medium into an entertainment one. But if we, as an artists and educators, do this we pay a dear price.

One of the most touching articles I have read in recent years is by a man who was one of the giants of band marching competition in Southern California. At the end of his life, he looked back at what he had given his life for.

> Looking back over my 69 years of being a band director, I see a pattern that made up my life. I came into the field because of the applause performance gives ...
>
> The most disturbing confession comes with the question: Was I really a music educator or had I chosen to specialize in the marching field because more people would see my band at one halftime show in the Los Angeles Coliseum than would see it in a lifetime of concert performances?
>
> I never had to defend my showmanship position. Everyone was delighted with the band program. However, I kept trying to defend it for myself. In those contemplative moments, I would rationalize by focusing on the tremendous experience my students enjoyed performing before thousands of spectators and a huge national television audience. Wasn't this the assignment of a music educator?
>
> Perhaps, but what about preparing my students to become consumers of good music after graduation? When had I given them a preview of the music of the masters? ... Why had competition become the curriculum of my band?[78]

78 Jack Mercer, 'Confessions of a Sixty-Nine-Year-Old Band Director,' *Today's Music Educator*, Fall, 1992.

Wagner, himself, paints a very bleak picture of the price the artist must pay if he elects to depart from the highest ideals of art. It is as if he were predicting the tragedy of just such a case as this band director.

> The man who strays into the realm of triviality must pay for his transgression at the cost of his own more noble nature;—but he who seeks it deliberately, that man is—fortunate, for he has *nothing* worth losing.[79]

[79] Letter to Eduard Hanslick, January 1, 1847, quoted in Steward Spencer and Barry Millington, *Selected Letters of Richard Wagner* (London: Dent), 135.

Thus, it is always a shock when a young instrumental music education major leaves our isolated university art world and discovers what the public really thinks of us. One of these young people recently wrote a very poignant letter on this subject.

> It seems that educators do not rate the same status as other 'professionals;' and as for music educators—well, the image is even more bleak. We are viewed as entertainers, not as 'real' teachers. Why?[80]

[80] Michele Heaphy, 'I'm a Teacher. I Teach Band,' *Band Directors Guide*, March/April, 1992.

The entertainment industry in the United States is already enormous. Can school music programs really offer the public entertainment comparable with the other media? The more important question is, of course, *should* we? Liszt says the answer must be No.

> The word 'Evening entertainment' must, as is self-evident, be entirely dispensed with. Our business is to raise, to educate the audience, not to amuse them.[81]

[81] Letter to an Unknown Person, Spring, 1859.

But if we decide it is *not* the role of the public schools to entertain the public, and it is our wish to devote our time with the students to aesthetic musical experiences, then the question follows: Will the public respond to *quality*? For me, the answer to that question has been clearly documented by the history of the modern orchestra and band. It was only after 1815 that the public for the first time began to hear regular concerts by bands and orchestras. One can imagine how exhilarating it must have been for the players of that period, to suddenly be performing before thousands of listeners instead of a small handful of aristocrats.

About mid-century both orchestras and bands began to attempt to enlarge their audiences by performing some 'popular' music, in the form of waltzes, gallops, mazurkas, marches, etc. But soon orchestras simply stopped playing this kind of music and focused their repertoire on aesthetic music. Bands, on the other hand, kept on trying to enlarge their audiences by playing lower and lower levels of music. This continued until the mid-twentieth century (I remember playing in public, as a junior high school student, band compositions with titles such as 'The One-armed Paper Hanger'). The interesting thing is that today orchestras have much larger audiences than bands, and they have done it by playing only the finest music!

Wagner, who witnessed this first period of large public audiences, observed that the audience comes to music utterly uneducated, but through repeated exposure to the finest music they are educated to a higher refinement of taste.[82] This is how we help educate the public. When we make our choices of the music we will use with our students, we are at the very same time educating the parents and public. The public *will* place a value on our programs based on what we set before them. But, Wagner cautions that we can not expect the public at large to place a higher value on what we are doing than we ourselves place on it.

[82] Letter to Hans von Bulow, December 27, 1868; and, 'Report to the Dresden *Abendzeitung*,' April 6, 1841.

> It has been said that Dresden had too many visitors, and others, who would never know what to do with themselves on an evening when there was no theatre. In my opinion this reply involves the bitterest condemnation of the prevailing estimate of the Theatre. So, only when people don't know what to do with a tiresome evening, will they go to the theatre? In effect, with a large section of the public this view has become a habit, and the Theatre accordingly has sunk to a mere source of entertainment, a pastime as surrogate for playing cards and so forth. If we do not start with a far greater and worthier opinion of the Theatre, and seek to bring it to common acceptance, we fail to see by what right we could ever demand the active support of the nation for this institution.[83]

[83] Quoted in Ellis, op. cit., VII, 335.

Liszt once wrote a beautiful thought in this regard, a plea to all of us to think higher.

> Let us ... cast out all but the noblest ambitions, to concentrate our concerns on efforts that dig a deeper furrow than the fashion of the day! Let us renounce, too, for ourselves, in the dreary time in which we live, all that is unworthy of art, all that lacks permanence, all that fails to shelter some grain of eternal and immaterial beauty which art must lighten gloriously in order to glow itself, and let us remember the ancient prayer of the Dorians, whose simple formula was so reverently poetic when they petitioned the gods: 'to give them Good through Beauty!' Instead of laboring so to attract and please listeners at any price, let us rather strive ... to leave a celestial echo of what we have

> felt, loved, and endured! Let us learn ... to demand of ourselves whatever ennobles in the mystical city of art rather than to seek from the present, without regard to the future, those easy crowns which, scarce assumed, are at once dulled and forgotten![84]

[84] Franz Liszt, *Chopin* (1852).

This 'support of the nation,' which Wagner was concerned about above, is certainly our concern as well. If we have music programs which teach children to love and appreciate great music, I believe they will continue to love and appreciate great music as adults. On the other hand, if our school music programs consist only as activities, then we lose these students when they become adults if for no other reason because these activities do not exist for adults.

It takes great courage and conviction to pursue the highest goals of music education at a time when the broad public is so easily satisfied by a diet of only entertainment. No one knew this better than Wagner.

> To take a last look back upon the picture afforded us by the Public ... we might compare it with a river, as to which we must decide whether we will swim against or with its stream. Who swims with it, may imagine he belongs to constant progress; because it is so easy to be borne along, and he never notices that he is being swallowed in the ocean of vulgarity. To swim against the stream must seem ridiculous to those not driven by an irresistible force to the immense exertions that it costs.[85]

[85] ibid., VI, 94.

8 *Epilogue*

WHEN ONE CONSIDERS THE LONG HISTORY of music and music education two themes clearly stand out in all places and in all times.

First, the central purpose of music has always been a special language of feelings. That truth remains unquestioned even when music is used in a secondary role for functional purposes.

Two, the central value in music education has been the ability of music to shape the character of the student and for this reason it was self-evident that only the highest quality music should be used in education. According to Plato this was recognized ten thousand years before his time and it was a self-evident Truth until shortly after 1950.

After 1950, in the United States, the doctors of higher education in music education called for a dramatic reversal in this long history. They created a philosophy under which music education was not based on music but rather on concepts about music. In a classic example of egalitarianism setting aside the obvious, they also declared that in music education all music is equal.

After fifty years of this abrupt departure from ages of practice in music education, what have these doctors of higher education given us? Today more students are learning music by themselves in their own homes with electronic toys than in our classrooms. And with their abandonment of their role in shaping the character of the student, what affect has music had on society during the past fifty years?

The purpose of these three books (*Philosophic Foundations of Education*, *Foundations of Music Education* and *Music Education of the Future*) has been to remind the reader of the long and noble history of music education in Western society. Armed with this knowledge of our cultural heritage we hope the reader will gain the confidence to form their own views on the value and practice of music education and the courage to break free from the current dogma. We urge music teachers to begin, as they look to the future, by reflecting on the two principles upon which music education was based for thousands of years:

If music consists of a language of feeling, then feeling must be the language of music education.

If the contribution to society by music education lies in the shaping of the character of the student, then it follows that the quality of that education cannot be divorced from the quality of the music it employs.

Dr. David Whitwell conducting in Laupheim, Germany, 2006

Illustrations

All artwork, illustrations, and photographs are either in the public domain or covered by a Creative Commons licence. Details of each illustration are below.

On The Roots of Music Education
A portrait of 31-year-old Charles Darwin by George Richmond (1809–1896) in 1840, public domain • Bone flute dated in the Upper Paleolithic from Geissenklösterle, a german cave on the Swabian region, Replica, Attribution: José-Manuel Benito Álvarez, License: Creative Commons Attribution-Share Alike 2.5 Generic • Photograph of composer Richard Wagner, Paris, 1861, by Pierre Petit (1832–1909), Source: Third party reproduction from Die Bildnisse Richard Wagners (The Portraits of Richard Wagner), a 1970 publication reproducing all the known portraits (photographs, drawings, paintings, likenesses) of Wagner made during his lifetime (1813-1883); Charles Ferdinand Reinwald, commissioner of the French Library wrote that this photo was first published in Théodore Pelloquet (ed), Galerie des hommes du jour (Gallery of the Men of the Days), public domain • Réflexions critiques sur la poésie et la peinture (Critical Reflections on Poetry and Literature) by French diplomat and historian Jean-Baptiste Dubos (1670–1742), 1755 (1st edition 1719), public domain • Portrait bust of William Shenstone (1714–1763) from the Frontispiece of The Works in Verse and Prose of William Shenstone, Esq., Vol. I, Second Edition (London, J Dodsley, 1765), public domain • Abbey of Solesmes, seen since the Port of Solesmes, Sarthe, France, Author: Cliatop, public domain • Gregorian chants for the night office of Christmas, 1895, Source Liber Responsorialis pro Festis I. Classis et Communi Sanctorum juxta Ritum Monasticum, Monastery of Solesmes, public domain • Woman with a lyre near an altar; a basket (?) on the left. Tondo of an Attic red-figure kylix, ca. 480 BC, Dubois Collection, De Ridder 581, Lower floor, smaller room, Source/Photographer: Marie-Lan Nguyen (2010), License: Creative Commons Attribution 2.5 Generic • Jean-Philippe Rameau (d. 1764), 18th C, public domain

Some Thoughts on the Perception of Music
Doctor Oliver Sacks at TED 2009, 5 February 2009, Author: Erik Charlton, License: Creative Commons Attribution 2.0 Generic • Maurice Ravel, public domain • Leonard Bernstein in rehearsal of his "Mass", 1971 Sept. 1, Source: United States Library of Congress's Prints and Photographs Division under the digital ID ppmsc.03255, public domain

Purpose and Meaning in Music Education
Medieval illustraion of Anicius Manlius Severinus Boëthius (a late-antique philosopher), public domain • Image from 1552 of Adrianus Petit Coclico, public domain • Caccini, le nuove musiche, License: GNU GNU GNU Free Documentation License, Creative Commons Attribution ShareAlike 3.0 • Arcangelo Corelli (1653-1713), public domain • Painting of Samuel Pepys by John Hayls (1600–1679) in 1666, public domain • Karajan, Herbert von: Dirigent, Generalmusikdirektor der Wiener Staatsoper, Österreich, 1941, Source: Deutsches Bundesarchiv (German Federal Archive), Bild 183-R92264, Thaler, E., This image was provided to Wikimedia Commons by the German Federal Archive (Deutsches Bundesarchiv) as part of a cooperation project. The German Federal Archive guarantees an authentic representation only using the originals (negative and/or positive), resp. the digitalization of the originals as provided by the Digital Image Archive, License: Creative Commons Attribution-Share Alike 3.0 Germany

The Focus of Music Education of the Future Must be Experiential and not Conceptual
English playwright, poet, and actor Ben Jonson (1572–1637) by George Vertue (1684–1786) after Gerard van Honthorst (1590–1656), 1730, Source: United States Library of Congress's Prints and Photographs division under the digital ID cph.3c16190, public domain • Robert Schumann, Wien 1839, Source: Lithographie by Joseph Kriehuber (1800–1876) , public domain • Gustav Mahler, 1860–1911; 3/4, seated, facing left, Copyright was registered in 1909–03–16 under H 124096–124098 by the studio A. Dupont, N.Y., Source: United States Library of Congress's Prints and Photographs division under the digital ID cph.3a00825, public domain • Woodcut showing Pythagoras with bells, a kind of glass harmonica, a monochord and (organ?) pipes in Pythagorean tuning. From Theorica musicae by Franchino Gaffurio, 1492 (1480?), public domain • Critica Musica by Johann Mattheson, public domain • Image of English 18th C. composer Charles Avison, public domain • Aaron Copland, License: This work is in the public domain in the United States because it is a work of the United States Federal Government under the terms of Title 17, Chapter 1, Section 105 of the US Code

The Music Education of the Future Must Educate All Children
no illustrations

Music Education of the Future Must Educate the Real Child
Abraham Maslow photograph, License: GNU GNU GNU Free Documentation License, Creative Commons Attribution-Share Alike 3.0 Unported • John Dickinson (1732–1808) of Delaware from Scharf, Thomas J. (1888), History of Delaware, 1609–1888, public domain • George Washington, 1795, Oil on canvas by Gilbert Charles Stuart (1755–1828), The Metropolitan Museum of Art, public domain • Opening notes of Mozart, Symphony No. 40, last movement, made with Sibelius 3 software by Opus33, public domain • French composer, violinist and conductor François-Antoine Habeneck (1781–1849), Source: Bibliothèque nationale de France, Author: Lange. P. C. Van Geel, Paris, public domain • Felix Weingartner by Julius Cornelius Schaarwächter (1847–1904) c. 1900, Source: Portrait Collection Friedrich Nicolas Manskopf at the library of the Johann Wolfgang Goethe-University Frankfurt am Main, public domain • German-born conductor and composer Bruno Walter (1876–1962), Source: United States Library of Congress's Prints and Photographs division (George Grantham Bain Collection) under the digital ID ggbain.33780, public domain • Hymn to Applo in Delphi, Greece (musical notation), Photo by Ziggur, public domain • Leonardo da Vinci (1452–1519), portrait of Musician Franchino Gaffurio, Milan, Pinacoteca Ambrosiana, c. 1490, also attributed to Giovanni Ambrogio de Predis, public domain • Portrait of Giuseppe Verdi by Giovanni Boldini (1842–1931), 1886, National Gallery of

Modern Art, Rome, public domain • Capa do VIII III III livro de madrigais, 1638, Source: Claudio Monteverdi, série Mestres da Música, ed. Abril São Paulo, 1979, public domain • Emile Jaques-Dalcroze, 1912, public domain • Carl Maria von Weber, public domain • Conductor Lorin Maazel, Author: Barbara Haws/Chris Lee, License: Creative Commons Attribution-Share Alike 2.5 Generic, GNU GNU GNU Free Documentation License, Creative Commons Attribution-Share Alike 3.0 Unported, Creative Commons Attribution 2.5 Generic

MUSIC EDUCATION OF THE FUTURE: TWO PARAMOUNT NEW PURPOSES

Martin Luther, "Bibliothek des allgemeinen und praktischen Wissens. Bd. 5" (1905), Deutsche Literaturgeschichte, Seite 57, public domain • Sergiu Celibidache, Sergiu Celibidache giving a conducting lesson at The Curtis Institute in 1984 to David Bernard, public domain • The Temple to Apollo, 28 May 2005, Author: Frank Fleschner, License: Creative Commons Attribution 2.0 Generic license • Robert G. Ingersoll, Library of Congress description: "Ingersoll, Robert (The Infidel)", Date between 1865 and 1880, Source: Library of Congress Prints and Photographs Division, Brady-Handy Photograph Collection., public domain • Hans Christian Anderson, Statue of Hans Christian Anderson in Solvang Park, 15 January 2010, public domain • Felix Mendelssohn Bartholdy at the age of 30 in London watercolor

About the Author

Dr. David Whitwell is a graduate ('with distinction') of the University of Michigan and the Catholic University of America, Washington DC (PhD, Musicology, Distinguished Alumni Award, 2000) and has studied conducting with Eugene Ormandy and at the Akademie fur Musik, Vienna. Prior to coming to Northridge, Dr. Whitwell participated in concerts throughout the United States and Asia as Associate First Horn in the USAF Band and Orchestra in Washington DC, and in recitals throughout South America in cooperation with the United States State Department.

At the California State University, Northridge, which is in Los Angeles, Dr. Whitwell developed the CSUN Wind Ensemble into an ensemble of international reputation, with international tours to Europe in 1981 and 1989 and to Japan in 1984. The CSUN Wind Ensemble has made professional studio recordings for BBC (London), the Koln Westdeutscher Rundfunk (Germany), NOS National Radio (The Netherlands), Zurich Radio (Switzerland), the Television Broadcasting System (Japan) as well as for the United States State Department for broadcast on its 'Voice of America' program. The CSUN Wind Ensemble's recording with the Mirecourt Trio in 1982 was named the 'Record of the Year' by The Village Voice. Composers who have guest conducted Whitwell's ensembles include Aaron Copland, Ernest Krenek, Alan Hovhaness, Morton Gould, Karel Husa, Frank Erickson and Vaclav Nelhybel.

Dr. Whitwell has been a guest professor in 100 different universities and conservatories throughout the United States and in 23 foreign countries (most recently in China, in an elite school housed in the Forbidden City). Guest conducting experiences have included the Philadelphia Orchestra, Seattle Symphony Orchestra, the Czech Radio Orchestras of Brno and Bratislava, The National Youth Orchestra of Israel, as well as resident wind ensembles in Russia, Israel, Austria, Switzerland, Germany, England, Wales, The Netherlands, Portugal, Peru, Korea, Japan, Taiwan, Canada and the United States.

He is a past president of the College Band Directors National Association, a member of the Prasidium of the International Society for the Promotion of Band Music, and was a member of the founding board of directors of the World Association for Symphonic Bands and Ensembles (WASBE). In 1964 he was made an honorary life member of Kappa Kappa Psi, a national professional music fraternity. In September, 2001, he was a delegate to the UNESCO Conference on Global Music in Tokyo. He has been knighted by sovereign organizations in France, Portugal and Scotland and has been awarded the gold medal of Kerkrade, The Netherlands, and the silver medal of Wangen, Germany, the highest honor given wind conductors in the United States, the medal of the Academy of Wind and Percussion Arts (National Band Association) and the highest honor given wind conductors in Austria, the gold medal of the Austrian Band Association. He is a member of the Hall of Fame of the California Music Educators Association.

Dr. Whitwell's publications include more than 127 articles on wind literature including publications in Music and Letters (London), the London Musical Times, the Mozart-Jahrbuch (Salzburg), and 39 books, among which is his 13-volume *History and Literature of the Wind Band and Wind Ensemble* and an 8-volume series on *Aesthetics in Music*. In addition to numerous modern editions of early wind band music his original compositions include 5 symphonies.

David Whitwell was named as one of six men who have determined the course of American bands during the second half of the 20th century, in the definitive history, *The Twentieth Century American Wind Band* (Meredith Music).

A doctoral dissertation by German Gonzales (2007, Arizona State University) is dedicated to the life and conducting career of David Whitwell through the year 1977. David Whitwell is one of nine men described by Paula A. Crider in *The Conductor's Legacy* (Chicago: GIA, 2010) as 'the legendary conductors' of the 20th century.

> 'I can't imagine the 2nd half of the 20th century—without David Whitwell and what he has given to all of the rest of us.' Frederick Fennell (1993)

www.ingramcontent.com/pod-product-compliance
Lightning Source LLC
Chambersburg PA
CBHW081217230426
43666CB00015B/2766